MW01620375

ICE AGE CIVILIZATIONS

JAMES I. NIENHUIS

HOUSTON, TEXAS
2006

Copyright © 2006 by James I. Nienhuis

All rights reserved. No part of this book may be reproduced or transmitted in any form or by any means, electronic or mechanical. This includes photocopying or recording by any information storage or retrieval system, without written permission from the publisher.

WWW.GENESISVERACITY.COM

Genesis Veracity
P.O. Box 850
5773 Woodway Drive
Houston, Texas 77057
1-866-GEOFACT

ISBN Number: 0-9726206-2-1

Library of Congress Cataloguing in Publication Data

Nienhuis, James I. — 1954
Ice Age Civilizations / by James I. Nienhuis. — 1st ed.
p. cm.
Includes Bibliographical References

1. Geology 2. Natural Selection 3. Ice Age
4. Astronomy 5. Human Evolution
6. Biblical History 7. Archaeology

The Book Connection Consultants
Book Design & Layout — Rita Mills
Cover art by Gladys Ramirez
Cover design by James I. Nienhuis

The paper used in this publication meets the requirements of the American National Standard for Permanence of Paper for Printed Library Materials Z39.48-1984.

Printed in the United States of America

Table of Contents

Introduction

The precise measurements and religious observances of the apparent movements of the sun and constellations of stars, in their orderly and predictable courses in the sky, was a great passion for the ancients, and such is reflected in their legends, megalithic buildings, and navigation maps, which reveal the ancients' awareness of the solar equinoxes and solstices, and also, which reveal that they actually measured the precession of the earth's axis, the slow gyroscope-like wobble of the earth's axis in space, that would cycle once in 25,920 years.

Those ancients could measure the earth with this knowledge because it allowed them to accurately calculate the radius and, so then, the circumference of the earth, and thereby, they were prepared to execute measurements for the accurate mapping and navigation of much of the globe within a few centuries during the Ice Age. Their star-mapping techniques allowed them to locate geographical points on the earth by measurements of the apparent movement of the locations of constellations from year to year, relative to the circle of the horizon, this apparent movement of the constellations is the visible manifestation of the earth's slow wobble, like a gyroscope in space.

The Great Pyramid of Giza in Egypt is an embodiment of their ancient earth-measuring capabilities, and its astronomically-derived dimensions reveal the ancients' precession-measuring, and thereby, their earth-measuring capabilities. The Great Pyramid is on the ancient Prime Meridian (Greenwich England is on today's Prime Meridian), and so, the mapping and surveying in ancient times was with the Great Pyramid as the geographical base reference-point, and therewith, ancient megalithic sites are at key precession-derived distances away from the Great Pyramid.

Some ancient maps, to be discussed, prove that the ancients were mapping and navigating the globe during the Ice Age. So then, should we actually believe that this occurred before 10000 B.C., when cavemen were supposedly just learning to farm with stone tools and live in crude villages, and also (ostensibly), to build large seaworthy vessels with precise navigation equipment to navigate and chart much of the globe? Advanced navigation and mapping doesn't really come to mind when one considers the image of the "cavemen" of pop archaeology.

Supposedly anomalous ancient submerged megalithic constructions are found resting on shallow seafloors near the shorelines in various parts of the world, and with the popular notion that the Ice Age ended around 10000 B.C., it follows that these well-designed and obviously manmade structures of massive hewed and fitted megaliths were built before then, before the end of the Ice Age, and when the Ice Age ended, the snow and ice melted and poured into the sea, to raise sea level a few hundred feet for the submergence of roughly 25 million square miles of land.

Mainstream scientists have a major quandary here, should they say that mankind has been navigating the high seas and building advanced megalithic structures since before 10000 B.C., the orthodox timeframe for the end of the Ice Age, or should they say that the Ice Age actually ended after their own date of circa 2000 B.C. for the characteristic forms and functions of these megalithic structures which are now on the seafloor?

The many confirmed submerged megalithic structures, which are found off the coasts of Malta, Egypt, Greece, Lebanon, Spain, India, China, and Japan, are ignored or feebly rationalized by most mainstream scientists, so I urge you to rigorously investigate the reality of these submerged megaliths, and understand the implications of their presence on the seafloor. Great pictures of some of these submerged megaliths can be viewed at www.GrahamHancock.com and www.Morien-Institute.org, so please access these as you read.

The ancient navigation maps which we will analyze show accuracies of east-west distances (longitudes) which would not be matched until the late 1700's A.D., with the invention and use of Harrison's Chronometer, so the ancients were obviously measuring the earth with another instrument, which was the archaeometer, or Celtic Cross, a form of which are the pieces of an ancient measuring device known as the Dixon Relics which were discovered within the Great Pyramid in the 19th century by Piazzi Smith.

This Celtic Cross (the archaeometer) measuring device was a circular hub affixed to the center of a cross, which was memorialized with graveyard tombstones and jewelry designs, and which, in its original form and function, allowed the ancients to master the measurement of the earth, and thereby, feel a sense of empowerment because of their unusual knowledge about the special relationship of precession time to the dimensions of the earth.

The sun was worshipped as the life-giver by these ancients, who also saw cosmic drama being played-out in the apparent movement of the constellations because of precession, so when these sun worshipping measurers-of-the-earth navigated and settled the globe during the Ice Age, from their original homeland in the Middle East/Egypt, they built megalithic ceremonial tiered-plazas and pyramids which are astronomically aligned to measure the solstices and equinoxes of the sun, and they built stone-circles like Stonehenge which are celestial clocks, with which they marked the progress of the constellations' slow apparent movement along the circle of the horizon, caused by the slow wobble of the earth's axis, which would cycle once in 25,920 years.

Some of these structures are now on the seafloor because they were submerged when the sea level rose a few hundred feet when the Ice Age icepack melted to pour into the sea. At that time, the snow-blitz of the Ice Age had ended, along with the heavy rains in the middle latitudes, which had made the now-arid Sahara, Middle East, and Indus regions, well-watered grasslands and forests during the Ice Age, so that massive climate change, within a matter of decades at the close of the Ice Age, caused vast swaths of those previously lush lands to become deserts, and so, to depopulate significantly beginning at around 1500 B.C.

Think about it, why would those ancients choose to initially settle in environments such as those of present day Egypt, the Middle East, and northwest India, which are now mostly parched desert wastelands? They settled in these regions because, before about 1500 B.C., these lands were lush and fruitful, and admittedly near big rivers, but the civilizations in those regions of Egypt, Sumer (Babylon), Elam (Persia), and the Indus-Sarasvati, declined rapidly when the rainfall precipitously declined at the end of the Ice Age, when even the Sarasvati River which was the life-blood of the Indus-Sarasvati civilization dried-up, and when the fruitful grasslands and forests of these earliest ancient civilizations became the desolate deserts which they are today.

Thank you for coming along for this ride, and I trust that the evidences presented herewith will cause you to reconsider the popularly held notions about our ancient history which are stubbornly adhered to by mainstream academicians. Keep in mind that mainstream scientists also cannot explain the cause of the Ice Age, so we will explore its necessitated cause as we analyze the origins and early migrations of humankind.

1
CHAPTER

Partially Submarine Kingdoms

Just offshore from the megalithic ruins of the ancient civilizations found in Egypt, on Malta (of the Minoan-Phoenician civilization), in India (of the Tamil and Indus-Sarasvati civilizations), and on Taiwan/Japan (of the Jomon civilization), there on the shallow seafloors, are found megalithic ruins which look like those still onshore.

One logically should deduce that all of these structures, both onshore and submerged, were built by these respective civilizations, and subsequently, some of their buildings were submerged when the Ice Age ended and sea level rose a few hundred feet while these civilizations were flourishing, but they then were forced to adjust to the end of the Ice Age, with its greatly reduced rainfall and risen sea level, the time of mass migrations of people groups, known by archaeologists to have occurred at around 1500 B.C.

The ancient Indus-Sarasvati civilization of eastern Pakistan and northwest India is reputed to have been founded and flourished circa 2000 B.C., with cities of high-quality mud-brick and megalithic rock-buildings that were gridded with precise networks of streets, and sanitation pipelines, and with ceremonial fire altars, and stone-circles for astronomical observations. Two cities have been discovered along an ancient river bed there in the Gulf of Cambay, about forty miles from shore in about 100 feet of water that have the same form and function as do those onshore at Mohenjo-Daro, Harappa, and Lothal, which are generally considered to be of 2000 B.C. vintage, so both the submerged and onshore cities' structures should be considered to have been constructed circa 2000 B.C., as they are of the same style.

Sonar scans of these two now submerged cities along a submerged river bed of the ancient Indus-Sarasvati civilization in the Gulf of Cambay show their dimensions (about two miles by about five miles long), and the scans show their buildings' forms which are like those on land, and Indus-Sarasvati civilization pottery and tools have been dredged up from these submerged cities,[1] but photographs may not be in the offing because the water there is very muddy and turbulent. Pictures of the sonar scan of the cities and their relics are provided by archaeological journalist Graham Hancock in his book *Underworld*[2] and at his website, which detail and provide photographs of many other submerged megaliths from the various parts of the world.

Hancock has produced voluminous research about the precise navigational mapping achieved by the ancients during the Ice Age, and about the submerged megaliths which must have been built before the end of the Ice Age, but he then torturously deduces that this proves that many of the great megalithic structures of the world must have been built before 10000 B.C., which is the commonly held date for the end of the Ice Age, and so therewith, the ancients must have also been sailing and mapping the globe with great precision, also before 10000 B.C., as reflected with the fantastically accurate ancient navigational maps which show Ice Age shorelines before sea level had risen a few hundred feet when the Ice Age icepack had melted.

However, he admits (with a muted voice of contrition) that the submerged megaliths at all these locations seem to be of the same form and function as those nearby onshore megalithic ruins which are commonly dated to around 2000 B.C., and so, he has reluctantly highlighted the contradiction between the orthodox date for the end of the Ice Age at around 10000 B.C. and the obvious 2000 B.C. vintage of the onshore and now-submerged megaliths.

In this catch twenty-two situation, mainstream scientists are forced to either disavow the submerged megaliths, or say that they were built before 10000 B.C. Obviously, neither is a palatable choice for the defenders of the archaeological status quo, because these same defenders of orthodox dogma correctly note that megalithic-building civilizations like Egypt, Sumer, and the Indus-Sarasvati sprang-up quickly at around 2000 B.C., although they would probably say closer to 3000 B.C., and so, these defenders of the archaeological status quo have also highlighted the contradiction between the orthodox date of the end of the Ice Age at around 10000 B.C., and their acknowledged date for the sudden appearance of megalithic building at circa 2000 B.C. (back to 3000 B.C in their book).

Another city of the ancient Indus-Sarasvati civilization was old Dwarka which is now on the seafloor, just offshore from modern-day Dwarka. The now submerged ancient Dwarka was about fifty miles inland during the Ice Age, on the Gomati River, but then the sea level rose about 300 feet to submerge its buildings which are of similar appearance to those later built at the second Dwarka, on the risen-ocean shoreline, such as long intersecting walls of interlocking L-shaped megalithic blocks (which also characterize the stone citadels on either side of the Gomati River of the submerged site) that were built after the sea level had risen to the present,[3] and fifty miles more inland, shoreline on which was built this post-Ice Age Dwarka.

The fact that the submergence of ancient Dwarka is recorded in an ancient history book which is much more likely to have been spawned near 2000 B.C., according to almost all the experts, rather than near 10000 B.C., when cavemen were supposedly just coming out of their caves, lends great credence to the notion that the Ice Age did end during the flourishing of this ancient Indus civilization circa 1500 B.C.

This same prodigious ancient sea level rise is described in the legends of the Tamils of southern India, who wrote that a land-bridge extended between Ceylon (Sri Lanka) and the southern tip of India, when the ancient kingdom of Kumari Kandam existed there in that now submerged land, with its now submerged Prahuli River drainage system and its now submerged rolling low hills including Mount Kumari (no doubt just a hill) which were engulfed when the Ice Age ended[4] and water poured into the oceans from the melting Ice Age icepacks to raise sea level by about 300 hundred feet.

Divers have described a temple on the seafloor that is one of many buildings there which are like the column-surrounded pyramid/pagoda which is onshore at Mahabalipuram of southeastern India, and those submerged megalithic constructions of offshore Mahabalipuram were observed when the tide went out, just before the great tsunami of December 2004 hit that coast, so the presence of these structures is unquestionable, yet orthodox scientists refuse to investigate.

According to Tamil legend, the buildings for the ancient school on Kumari Kandam were engulfed by the sea, 1850 years before the most recent school's end at around 350 A.D., in its most recent megalithic building which was constructed on the new shoreline after the sea level had risen to its current post-Ice Age level.[5] Simple arithmetic says that the sea level therefore rose circa 1500 B.C. at the end of the Ice Age. So we see that the local ancient records of the people of India do corroborate the commonality of architectural motifs' between their submerged and their onshore megaliths which are commonly dated to around 2000 B.C.

The shoreline city Kaniya Kumari on the extreme tip of southern India was built as a monument to the completed sea level rise at the end of the Ice Age, according to the ancient Kumari Kandam legends, and the Indian Sanskrit epic Ramayana describes the sea level rise which covered the now shallow seafloor off the coast of southern India which was the land of the kingdom of Kumari Kandam, so the ancients are again indirectly telling us that the Ice Age ended when their earliest institutions of learning and their most ancient temples were engulfed by the risen sea level. To corroborate this account, the ancient Tamil poem Kalittogai describes that the ancient Pandiyan king Nediyon had to flee Kumari Kandam and conquer lands to the north because the sea level had risen to engulf the land of his first kingdom.[6] Incidentally, Kumari Kandam means virgin country, where lived some of their earliest ancestors, such as kings Nediyon, Bali, and Ravanna.

Hancock would have us believe that all these stories about the submergence of vast tracts of land are from around 10000 B.C., the date that orthodox scientists say that the Ice Age ended, and when cavemen were supposedly just coming out of their caves to begin to farm the land with crude stone tools. And mainstream academicians would have us believe that all these stories, which they choose not to investigate, are vain imaginations from ancient storytellers with bizarrely vivid and foolish imaginations, so obviously, both of their rationales about the evidences for the time of the end of the Ice Age fall far short of the mark for explanatory value and for an ideally honest investigation of these evidences.

Computer simulations by Glenn Milne which display the lower sea level during the Ice Age show that these portions of the now shallow seafloor off southern India were in fact exposed land during the Ice Age, and a vast swath of the now shallow seafloor off the coast of northwest India, upon which the submerged Indus-Sarasvati civilization cities rest, was then dry land. The then exposed land of southern India extended a few hundred miles up the southeastern coast of India, so submerged megaliths have also been reported off Chennai (Madras), Poompuhur, and Mahabalipuram, this was all part of the kingdom of Kumari Kandam, which succumbed to a crazy encroaching ocean circa 1500 B.C.[7]

The sea level rose about 300 feet around India and around other middle latitude landmasses of the earth, and it rose less than that in the more northerly latitudes around the continental landmasses which carried Ice Age icepacks up to two miles deep. The weight of the Ice Age icepack on North America, on northern and eastern Europe, and on Siberia, pushed down the underlying continental landmasses, but when the Ice Age icepack melted and poured into the oceans, the icepack overburden on these continental landmasses was relieved, so these relieved landmasses rose roughly 100 feet while the sea level was rising, such that the net sea level rise was less than was the rise around the landmasses in the middle latitudes which are far away from the continental regions which were relieved of their Ice Age icepack overburdens (on northern Europe and Asia, and on the Himalayas, the Andes, the Alps, and other major mountain chains).

This phenomenon of the continental crust's rebound in response to the removal of the overburden is known as isostatic rebound, and it is one reason why much of the 25 million square miles of land which was submerged at the end of the Ice Age are in the middle latitudes. The other reason is that the seas of southern Asia are generally shallower than the seas around Europe and northern Asia, and so, much more land was exposed in southern Asia when the sea level was about 300 feet lower during the Ice Age.

The submerged megaliths off southern India serve the local fishermen well, as those walls and temples provide rare bottom structure on the seafloor in that region which is gradually sloping and barren, so fish congregate around these seafloor anomalies in great numbers, and are predictably sought there by the local fishermen. The fishermen are constantly hanging their nets on these buildings, and must dive to loose the nets, when they see the columns, megalithic pyramids (pagodas), stone walls, inner rooms, and lion statues of the submerged kingdom of Kumari Kandam.[8]

It is not surprising that mainstream scientists see no reason to rally a small portion of their extensive resources to aggressively investigate these megalithic structures because it's a lose-lose affair for them. If they investigate these megaliths, they also should investigate the other submerged megaliths of the Indus-Sarasvati, Taiwan/Japan, Malta, Greece, Lebanon, Spain, and Egypt, so since this would be their inevitable and unpalatable task, and because they know that all of these megaliths cannot be explained away, they choose to do the old Sergeant Schultz from Hogan's Heroes and say "I see nuthink!"

Let me point out that some naysayers of the fact that these megaliths were submerged when the Ice Age ended and sea level rose hundreds of feet will baselessly insist that these megaliths were submerged because of earthquakes, but in fact, the geologic record in these areas of the world belie the notion that massive blocks (horsts and grabens) of seashore dropped into the ocean, and there are no ancient legends or writings about such events, so this argument is specious, and is a primary marker of mainstream science's desperation to explain away the all too apparent.

The ancient Jomon culture of Taiwan and Japan built megalithic tiered ceremonial plazas and stone-circles for astronomical science, some of which are now found on the seafloor as a result of the inundation of low-lying Jomon territory by the massive flood of melt-water into the ocean with the end of the Ice Age. The computer simulation of the lower sea level during the Ice Age confirms that these now submerged megaliths were then on dry land, so once again, the status quo purveyors of orthodoxy must explain away these megaliths, which are obviously manmade, as demonstrated with the vivid photographs of them in their clear water realm at www.GrahamHancock.com and www.Morien-Institute.org.

During the Ice Age, the present-day chain of Japanese islands was one long landmass trending northeast to southwest which connected to mainland China through Korea and perhaps Taiwan, and much of that long landmass was submerged at the end of the Ice Age, leaving the islands of Japan as the remnant of that sea level rise. The submerged megaliths are found and photographed offshore from the southwestern (Ryuku) islands of Japan near Okinawa, and they are of the same styles and functions as are those found proximally onshore.

The five precisely-tiered levels of the submerged Yonaguni complex in southwestern Japan defy any natural causation. If this stylized anomaly on this mudstone-rock underwater hillside of Yonaguni island was caused by erosion, then there should be rock debris resting below these precisely hewn ninety-degree lines of the tiers' horizontal edges which were supposedly formed by erosion, but no such erosion debris exists on the flat horizontal portions of the tiers below these ninety-degree cut horizontal edges.[9] The obvious conclusion is that this four-hundred foot-long and forty foot-tall multi-tiered complex was manmade, and was submerged when sea level rose because of the end of the Ice Age.

Archaeologists theorize from the evidence that the ancients cut megalithic structures with bronze saws, which were tipped with minerals harder than the megalith to be cut, and after a good starting cut was made in the rock, soaked wooden wedges were inserted into the saw-cut, so when the wedges dried and expanded, the rock split. It seems that the ancients of the Jomon culture hewed these structures at around 2000 B.C., because so-called cavemen couldn't have done it, and then some of the structures were submerged when the sea level rose to engulf roughly 25 million square miles of land worldwide at around 1500 B.C.

The markings of this saw-cut then wedge-and-separate rock-hewing technology are found of onshore megaliths and of submerged megaliths, so this technology was utilized during the Ice Age when these structures were built and before the Ice Age icepack had melted to raise the sea level a few hundred feet to engulf the low-lying buildings of this ancient Jomon culture of Japan, as well as of the ancient Tamil and Indus-Sarasvati cultures of India, and many others around the world. But to imagine such building being performed by cavemen who were just learning to farm with stone tools supposedly at 10000 B.C. stretches credulity to the limit, as even mainstream scientists propone that advanced megalithic building did not occur until around 2000 B.C., which is contradictorily some 8,000 years after their proposed time that the Ice Age ended.

In the waters off the island of Kerama near Yonaguni are found megalithic walls and stone-circles submerged at depths of 50 to 100 feet that look like those Jomon walls and stone-circles found onshore. The stone circle megaliths are carved out of the underlying rock, and are 10 feet high, and the circles of these carved megaliths are up to 50 feet across, and are aligned to measure the solar solstices and equinoxes,[10] so all this work was by crude cavemen who supposedly could barely rub two sticks together, and who had just figured-out how to plant seeds for farming?

The ancients were truly fascinated by the movements of the stars, planets, and sun, so they marked the equinoxes and solstitices of the sun with the alignments of the megalithic stones of these circles. And if these circles are like that at Stonehenge in England, the Jomon were also measuring the precession of the stars, and therewith, they were also revealing their anciently-rooted knowledge about the movement of the stars along the arch or circle of the sky, which allowed these ancients to measure and thereby map the arch or circle of the earth, as proven with the astronomically-derived dimensions of the Great Pyramid of Giza, and with the maps of the Ice Age mariners that show the Great Pyramid on the ancient Prime Meridian for their global mapping and navigating endeavours.

Ancient stone-circles and pyramids are found in many disparate parts of the globe, and their commonalities of forms and functions have flummoxed mainstream scientists for decades because the so-called races of people allegedly developed their cultures independently of each other, on their respective continents, after having migrated to those regions of the earth with a primitive and fledgling tool-making level of sophistication (crude stone arrowheads, scrapers, and "hand-axes"), and with only the pursuit of food and warmth on their minds. But why would these separately evolving cultures intentionally develop virtually the same megalithic building types as those from the other side of the globe whose respective builders had purportedly nothing in common except some supposed shared primitive hominid ancestors?

In the Mediterranean, submerged megaliths off Malta and Egypt are also being ignored by mainstream academicians because of the dire implications for their orthodox notions about ancient history. Submerged ancient roads, temples, stone-circles, and walls, have been found about five miles off the northern coast of Malta at Sliema on an underwater plateau in about forty feet of water. The plateau is about one-thousand feet by two-hundred feet in area, and on it, some of the constructions remain virtually intact, and there are many fallen megalithic blocks, as well.

These submerged megalithic structures look little different from those found on land at Hagar Qim, Tarxien, and Gigantija on Malta which are from around 2000 B.C. (some would say closer to 3000 B.C.), and since, according to the Ice Age sea level computer simulation maps by Milne, this now shallow seafloor north of Malta was dry land and connected to Sicily during the Ice Age, it is apparent that these buildings were constructed around the commonly accepted time of circa 2000 B.C., and some of them were then submerged when the Ice Age ended and sea level resultantly rose at around 1500 B.C., to engulf what was the peninsula which jutted south from southern Sicily, but then became the islands of Malta, because the higher elevations of this Ice Age peninsula from Sicily became islands when the sea level rose at the end of the Ice Age.

A diver described one megalithic temple on this underwater plateau near Sliema as follows:

> *The structure itself shows the same characteristics as the other above ground temples on Malta. Gigantic stone blocks aligned with astronomical significance, thought to be used as a calendar. The basic diameter of the interior rooms are 6 to 7 meters (about 20 feet) and some of the highest walls are still standing are about 4 to 6 meters (about 15 feet) high. There is an avenue that goes up the center of the structure indicating an orientation to the solar equinoxes. There are kidney-like formed rooms orientated to an easterly direction, which would coincide with the rising sun and the winter or summer solstices. The main difference is that this structure is underwater.*[11]

We see a glaring similarity among all these submerged megaliths from various regions of the earth, they all show striking resemblances to those megalithic constructions which are found just onshore. And as confirmed by the Ice Age sea level simulation maps, all of those now submerged lands on which the submerged megaliths rest were above sea level during the Ice Age, so the rational deduction is that the megaliths under discussion were all built around 2000 B.C., during the Ice Age, and those built on lower elevations during the Ice Age were submerged thereafter, when the melt-water at the end of the Ice Age poured into the sea for the sea level to rise a few hundred feet.

Also virtually ignored by mainstream scientists are the extensive seafloor megaliths off the coast of Egypt at Alexandria. In the Bay of Abu Kir near Alexandria in the Mediterranean are strewn the remains of columns and walls that were made of huge granite blocks which must have been transported some one-thousand miles from southern Egypt, and among the ruins are two small sphinx's along with other statues,[12] so we are again faced with this quandary, did the cavemen build these around 10000 B.C., or does the commonly held view that megalithic building began around 2000 B.C. hold true, and so, the Ice Age actually ended after 2000 B.C.?

On an underwater ridge surrounded by deeper water about three miles northeast of Alexandria in the Mediterranean Sea are the submerged megalithic walls of Sidi Gaber that consist of hundreds of huge same-sized (eight ft. x eight ft. x four ft.) hewn limestone blocks that were stacked three abreast and two high to form hundreds of feet of walls.[13] These structures are obviously not the random result of capricious and turbulent seas carrying massive and uniformly sculpted rock-blocks to this underwater ridge to magically agglomerate as precise and uniform walls.

The ancient Jewish historian Artapanus reported that at the time of the Exodus, the Nile River became stagnant and choked with rotting debris, as it seems that the sea level was rising circa 1500 B.C., and that rising sea level impeded the flow of the Nile into the Mediterranean, and so, the backed-up water of the Nile didn't flow as freely and became fetid because of stagnation and rotting creatures.[14] Many other natural disasters like the explosion of the volcanic island of Thera, and the Mount Etna of Sicily in the Mediterranean, were occurring around the world at that time because of the isostatic rebound of the earth's continental crust under the rapidly lessening Ice Age icepack overburden on the lands of the more extreme latitudes.

Located on an underwater plateau some four miles offshore from Alexandria in the Mediterranean are the submerged megaliths of Kinessa (which means Temple in Arabic). These now-submerged ruins of the ancient port city of Rahinet (the city known as Heraklieon by the Greeks) are well-known to the local fishermen for the structures' fish-attracting and unfortunate net-hanging character,[15] but mainstream scientists predictably see nothing here to investigate, and so, nothing to rationally explain, as they have from day one practiced dodge-and-weave tactics of obfuscation in dealing with the many known submerged megaliths of the various ancient civilizations.

Such is the out-of-sight, out-of-mind, intellectual approach which the purveyors of archaeological orthodoxy must project in hopes of avoidance of the clear implications of the reality of these submerged 2000 B.C. vintage megalithic constructions. Regional newspapers in the Mediterranean, and in India, Taiwan and Japan, have reported about these submerged megaliths (see Appendix IV), and yet, only a few renegade investigators like Graham Hancock have bothered to chronicle them in depth, and then to consider their mind-boggling ramifications for our notions about ancient history.

My hat is off to the alternative archaeological investigators, like Hancock, who have bucked orthodoxy through the documentation of these megalithic buildings on the seafloor, but their insistence that these now submerged megaliths were built at around 10000 B.C. is plainly baseless, and their failure to understand and admit that the evidence truly does indicate that the Ice Age ended at around 1500 B.C. reveals a nascent attachment to orthodoxy which even these alternative archeological expositors seem unable to shake off.

One of the biggest and certainly the most famous of the ancient megalithic structures which were built around 2000 B.C. is the Great Pyramid of Giza in Egypt. The Nile River flows from south to north across Egypt, and in northern Egypt, where the Nile diverges to become the sluggish streams of the triangular-shaped Nile Delta which flow into the Mediterranean, lie Cairo and the Great Pyramid of Giza, which is on the ancient Prime Meridian.

This massive ancient pyramid of astronomically-derived dimensions reveals the methodology for the mapping and navigating that was practiced by the ancients to sail to and map faraway lands like those of the Jomon of Japan, and as we shall see, the ancients were in fact mapping and navigating much of the earth during the Ice Age, because they could measure the dimensions of the earth with the "Celtic Cross."

2

CHAPTER

Wheel of Time Measured at Giza

The stars of the constellations appear to rotate extremely slowly along the horizon like a merry-go-round, or like a grinding wheel, because the earth's axis wobbles like a gyroscope in space, and would wobble once through a full cycle of precession in 25,920 years.

The ancients were able to measure this very slow earth axis wobble-caused apparent movement of constellations of the zodiacs' locations along the horizon at dawn on a given date from year to year with the Celtic Cross (the archaeometer), and yes, this is same Celtic Cross which has been the design for gravestones and jewelry.

The form of the Celtic Cross is memorialized in these designs because the ancient archaeometer was implemented by the ancients to measure the rate that this merry-go-round of the stars seems be move along the horizon, and thereby, to measure the radius of the earth, and therewith, the circumference of the earth, and thusly, they were able to measure (map) the earth, and this is proven with the astronomically-derived dimensions of the Great Pyramid of Giza in Egypt that rests on the ancient Prime Meridian.

The Celtic Cross (or archaeometer) is a calibrated cross with a calibrated wheel affixed to the center of that cross which is gravitationally oriented by a connected plumb-bob hanging from it. With this instrument, the ancients could measure the rate at which the precession of the earth's axis causes stars' locations on the horizon at dawn on a given date from year to year to appear to very slowly move along the horizon at the rate of 72 years to move 1 degree of 360 degrees.

The earth's axis is tilted as the earth moves in its counter-clockwise path around the sun during the course of a year, and this tilt of the earth's axis results in the changing seasons, as the earth moves in its annual path around the sun, spinning all the while to cause day and night. And the resultant clockwise-progressing series of the 12 constellations of the zodiac, on the horizon, are seen behind the rising sun as the tilted earth moves all the way around the sun during one year.

But because the very slow and opposite clockwise 25,920-year-wobble of the tilted earth's axis causes the constellations of the zodiac to seem to slightly shift along the horizon in a counter-clockwise direction, from dawn to dawn, on a given date through the years, the constellation of the zodiac which is behind the rising sun on a given date of the of year slowly transitions to the next constellation through 2,160 years (as 12 x 2,160 = 25,920).

Since the ancients knew that the length of one side of a hexagon (which is a six-sided polygon) is the same length as is the radius of a circle which circumscribes this hexagon, the ancients knew that if they could measure one side of the hexagon which is circumscribed by the circle of the earth, they could then determine the radius of the earth, and thusly, they could calculate the diameter and circumference of the earth, and so, with this capability, the ancients could measure and map the globe, as evidenced by the ancient navigational maps which will later be discussed.

By the measurements taken with the archaeometer, the ancients calculated that at the measured rate of the apparent movement of constellations' locations along the horizon from dawn to dawn on a given date through the years (72 years per 1 degree of 360 degrees), it would take 25,920 years for the constellations to seem to move, because of precession, all of the way around the horizon, that is one full circle, in a counter-clockwise direction, and so they calculated that the seeming movement of the stars along one side of the earth hexagon would take 1/6th of 25,920 years, or 4,320 years.

And with the archaeometer, the ancients geographically pinpointed the two ends of one side of the earth hexagon, because they could move from west to east, or from east to west, and calculate how far along the horizon would the constellations appear at dawn in the same position after 4,320 years of precession from their time, or how far along the horizon would the constellations have appeared in the same position 4,320 years before their time of the measurement.

To determine the distance between two geographical points which are separated by 1/6th of the earth's circumference, the ancient earth-measurers sighted a particular star near the horizon with the archaeometer, and then, another particular star was sighted near the horizon which was 60 degrees from the initial star, and so, according to the hexagon mapping scheme, the ancient navigators traveled to reach the geographical point on earth where the initial star was back-sighted, so to speak, to that same separation of 60 degrees from the second star sighted.

Having had determined two geographical points on the earth that represented the ends of one side of the earth hexagon, they then, also with the archaeometer, subdivided the length of the one side of the earth hexagon, and as it turns out, the perimeter length of the Great Pyramid is 1/7,200th of the length of one side of that hexagon which is circumscribed by the circle of the earth.

We know that they subdivided one side of the earth hexagon by 7,200 because the Great Pyramid's base perimeter length is 1/43,200th of the earth's circumference, and because 6 sides of the earth hexagon times the 7,200 subdivisions per one side of that earth hexagon equals 43,200 subdivisions of the earth's circumference, we see that each of the 7,200 subdivisions of one side of the earth hexagon is the length of the Great Pyramid's base perimeter.

And heretofore, the reason for the 20.632 inch length for the Egyptian royal cubit was the subject of mere conjecture, such as perhaps that the royal cubit is a standardized length for six or seven palm widths, or the length from a pharaoh's elbow to his fingertip. But such does not jibe with the fact that the astronomically-derived length of the Great Pyramid's base is 1,760 (4 x 440) royal cubits, so there obviously was a precession-measured basis for the royal cubit's length, and not some primitive hand measurement or forearm measurement as the basis for its length.

The 1,760 cubits around the base of the Great Pyramid times 20.632 inches/cubit gives us 36,309 inches, and when divided by 12 inches/foot gives us 3,026 feet, which is almost exactly half of the length of the 6,076 foot long nautical mile. And as the base perimeter-length of the Great Pyramid is 1/43,200th of the circumference of the earth, and as the length of the nautical mile is exactly half of that, being 1/21,600th of the circumference of the earth, we see that the length of the royal cubit was derived from precession measurements by the ancients.

The base perimeter-length of the Great Pyramid was obviously derived astronomically through the measurement of precession with the archaeometer, and with this Great Pyramid as the grand monument to the ancients' ability to measure the earth, it is not surprising that they were enabled to sail away from the Middle East during the Ice Age to map and settle much of the world, as demonstrated with the presence of ancient maritime civilizations throughout the world that also built megalithic structures, some of which, like Kinessa (Herakleion) and Sidi Gaber of Egpyt, were submerged when sea level rose at the end of the Ice Age.

This demonstrated earth-measuring capability of the ancients is the root of our modern mapping and timekeeping system, as evidenced by the fact that the modern nautical mile is exactly twice the length of the perimeter of the base of the Great Pyramid, so because the nautical mile would be almost exactly the same length as the Pyramid's perimeter-length if the ancients had subdivided the one side of the earth hexagon by 3,600 rather than by 7,200, it is apparent that the ancients actually founded our mapping and timekeeping system.

The circumference length of the earth is 21,600 nautical miles (arc seconds) because 360 degrees x 60 arc seconds/degree = 21,600 arc seconds, which are nautical miles, around the circumference of the earth, and this number 21,600 is half of the 43,200 base perimeter lengths of the Great Pyramid that equal the circumference of the earth, so the ancient and modern mapping and timekeeping systems are self-evidently one and the same, the only difference being that the ancients subdivided one side of the earth hexagon by 7,200, while we have subdivided it by 3,600 for the length of the nautical mile.

The number 360 degrees for the circle of the earth that circumscribed the earth hexagon was selected because each side of the earth hexagon was allotted a convenient base 6 number of degrees, which was decided to be 60, and when multiplied by the number 6 of sides of the earth hexagon, the 360 degree number results which is the base of our modern mapping and timekeeping system. Note again that there are 60 arc seconds per 1 degree, and each arc second is 1 nautical mile, which is exactly twice as long as the perimeter-length of the Great Pyramid, because the ancients sub-divided a side of the earth hexagon by 7,200, but not by 3,600, to establish the perimeter length for the Great Pyramid.

This Great Pyramid and ancient mapping finding is presented in full as Appendix 1 at the end of the book because I don't want the eyes of the non-mathematically-inclined to temporarily glaze over during the reading of this chapter, but I urge those and the rest to read it carefully to see that the finding does make sense, and to have some germane notions in the back of your mind that are integral to the further explanation of this ancient mapping phenomenon.

The Celtic Cross was named the archaeometer by its patent holder, Crichton Miller, who has successfully marketed this instrument as a back-up navigational device for mariners. He has congratulated me on this ancient mapping finding, and asked that I credit him for his work which contributed to my understanding of the ancients' accurate mapping by measurements of the precession of the axis of the earth which manifests as the constellations' seeming to move along the horizon through the years. Miller's website is www.CrichtonMiller.com, and you can there learn more about the Celtic Cross and its capabilities.

A press release from Mr. Miller is found in the back of this book as Appendix II (and see Appendix III), which I also urge you to read because it's a nice summary of the logical process which he employed to deduce the methodology and structure of this measuring device. And as mentioned in that press release, the catalyst which sparked Miller's intellectual quest to discover the methodology, which allowed the ancients to astronomically derive the dimensions for the Great Pyramid, was the discovery and his analysis of pieces of an ancient archaeometer which were discovered within the Great Pyramid, and are known as the Dixon Relics, and these are discussed at his website.

Because the ancients measured the earth, by linking time to distance through the measurement of precession, they were able to establish the precise locations of geographical reference points, by measuring with the archaeometer how many Great Pyramid perimeter-lengths (which are one-half of one nautical mile) that those geographical points were away from the Great Pyramid, and then, they located other geographical points near those established geographical reference points by measuring the time it took, at a known rate of speed, to get from the established location of a geographical reference point, to a near-to-it geographical point.

By noting their travel-time at a known rate of speed to the near geographical points from the already established geographical reference point, and by knowing their direction of travel from the sun's position, or from the angle which the Polestar made with the horizon, the ancients accurately mapped points near their respective established geographical reference points, and thereby, with much archaeometer work and extensive navigating, they accurately mapped much of the world during the Ice Age, as proven with the maps of the ancient sea kings.

3

CHAPTER

THEY MEASURED AND MAPPED THE GLOBE

Archaeologists and cartographical historians have for centuries been aware of medieval maps which were compiled during the1300's A.D. through the 1500's A.D. in Constantinople, Venice, and Portugal, that accurately locate the coastlines of Europe, Africa, the Americas, and even Antarctica (which supposedly wasn't discover until 1818 A.D. by the Russians).

Academicians, in avoidance of the obvious implications have, by and large, ignored these maps, which are fantastically accurate, and which amazingly reveal the coastlines of these landmasses as they were during the Ice Age, when the sea level was about 300 feet lower in the middle latitudes, and about 100 feet lower near where were the Ice Age icepack's massive overburdens on the continental landmasses in the more extreme latitudes, on North America, Northern Europe, and on Northern Asia, the Ice Age icepack had pushed down those continental landmasses into the mantle about two hundred feet, and so, when the Ice Age ended, those land-masses rebounded up, so sea level around those regions rose a net of only about 100 feet.

The Oronteus Finneus Map, compiled in 1513 A.D., even shows Antarctica, long before the Ice Age icepack had fully built-up on that landmass. This map accurately locates the mountain ranges, river valleys, and bays of that landmass, which are now thousands of feet under ice and snow, and so, the obvious implication is that those intrepid ancient mariners, who sailed to and mapped Antarctica, did so during the time that the Ice Age was in its early stages.[1]

Such does not mean that ancient mariners were plying the seas 200,000 years ago, which is a commonly held date for the beginning of the Ice Age, but it does mean that the Ice Age was actually in its early stages when the construction began of the great ancient megalithic buildings, such as those of Egypt, of the Indus/Sarasvati kingdom of northwest India, of the Kumari Kandam kingdom of southern India, and of the east Asian Jomon civilization.

Remember, this was the time when the ancients demonstrated their ability to measure and map the earth with their astronomically-derived dimensions for the construction of the Great Pyramid. And as the Great Pyramid is on the Prime Meridian of ancient times (Greenwich, England is on the modern Prime Meridian), the maps which we will analyze, that precisely locate the shorelines of these continents as they were during the Ice Age, reveal that the base geographical reference point for this entire precession-derived mapping system was the Great Pyramid of Giza in Egypt.

In his book *Maps of the Ancient Sea Kings*, author Charles Hapgood has published pictures of many of these medieval maps which, according to their medieval Turkish and Portuguese makers, were compilations of maps which were spirited away by the Franks from the great ancient Library at Alexandria in Egypt, to Constantinople in Turkey when that great Egyptian library, founded by Alexander the Great, was destroyed at around 600 A.D.

The medieval Turkish cartographers wrote on their maps that their source maps which had been recovered from the Library at Alexandria were very ancient, and were based upon mathematics and astronomy. They said that these source maps were made by the Tyranean Seafish of ancient Phoenicia,[2] and of course, there is more than bountiful evidence that the Phoenicians were sailing to many parts of the world for mining opportunities during their hey-day from around 2000 B.C. until around 500 B.C.

It is humorous that the Phoenicians would warn their precession-mapping-ignorant rivals to not venture too far by sea lest they fall off the edge of the earth, or lest they be eaten by dreadful sea creatures, and thusly, the Phoenicians retained their navigation superiority over their rivals, and they therefore had a virtual monopoly over far-flung mining operations and the transport of the metals.

The evidences of Phoenician mining operations in the Great Lakes region of North America, in the southern U.S., and in Australia, are abundant and well catalogued, but these are generally avoided by mainstream academicians because of their orthodox fixation that the ancestors of almost all of the North American and South American tribes came across the Bering Land Bridge between Asia and Alaska, on foot, during the Ice Age.

There is indeed abundant evidence that migrations occurred across that land bridge, when sea level was lower during the Ice Age, to expose a one thousand mile-wide land connection from Asia to North America, but that doesn't change the fact that orthodox archaeologists, by and large, have their heads in the sand about the evident ancient seafaring by the Phoenicians, and others, as we shall see.

Turkish Admiral Piri Reis produced a map in 1513 which displays the shoreline of the east coast of South America, and the shoreline of western Africa, and the Atlantic shoreline of Antarctica, with accuracies not to be matched until modern times.[3] Forming an arc on the map in the Atlantic Ocean are five established reference points which are radially equidistant from the Great Pyramid, which is on the ancient Prime Meridian.

Note that a landmark was not necessary to establish these reference points because the ancient navigators knew their accurate locations on the earth while at sea with the use of the archaeometer to triangulate the constellations, and with their knowledge of relative latitudes, according to the position of the sun on the horizon, or by measuring the angle between the Polestar (which essentially doesn't move) and the horizon directly under it, they could pinpoint geographic locations with amazing precision.

These established reference points were located in the Atlantic by measurements, with the archaeometer, of their equidistance from Giza, and by calculating their latitudes relative to the Great Pyramid's latitude, according to the relative angles of the Polestar with the horizon at the respective to-be-established reference points in the Atlantic, they thereby were able to accurately locate these reference points for their surveying of vast expanses of the globe.

(And in reality, the ancients could determine their locations by the positions of the constellations, with the archaeometer, without the measurement of the angle of the Polestar with the horizon.)

On the Piri Reis Map, lines are drawn radially from these five established reference points that intersect the coastlines of the landmasses, so through the knowledge of the direction and distance of the intersections of these radial lines with the coastlines from the established reference points, the ancient precession-measuring navigators were able to accurately map those points of intersections' locations on the globe because they could measure the earth, and so, they could calculate relative locations on the earth vis-à-vis the base reference point which was the Great Pyramid of Giza.

These maps were not drawn according to longitude and latitude because the shorelines were pinpointed by known lengths and directions of radial lines emanating from established reference points, which were established at radially equidistant locations from the Great Pyramid of the ancient Prime Meridian. The ancients' modus operandi for mapping was the knowledge of distance and direction, with east-west distance derived by earth measurements with the archaeometer, and north-south distances also by the measurements with the archaeometer (or by the measurement of the angle of the Polestar to the horizon, or by the relative position of the sun).

These medieval Turkish and Portuguese maps, which are compilations of the maps from the ancient Phoenician sea kings, are like overlapping modern polar projection maps, which are also radial projections, but which have the North and South Poles as the respective base reference points for those respective modern polar projection maps. The polar projections are as if you are looking directly down on either of the poles, so short radial projections of distance from a Pole will be accurately measured from directly above, but more distant radial projections of distance from a Pole will be less accurate, because the earth is curving away from the observer who is directly over that pole.

In order to, as accurately as possible, transfer spherical surface distance and direction data onto a flat-surface map, the ancient sailing cartographers of the Ice Age drew relatively small radial projection maps from the established reference points which were equidistant from Giza, and then they overlapped these smaller maps to become larger maps of larger regions. In fact, Piri Reis wrote on his map that it was a compilation of twenty maps which had been recovered from the Library at Alexandria that were said to have come from the ancient Tyranean Seafish of Phoenicia who, according to their accurately drawn shorelines of the world, were sailing the seas during the Ice Age.

The map made by the Turk Ibn Ben Zara in 1487 A.D., which was also compiled from ancient precession maps, shows very accurately the coastlines and islands of the Mediterranean. The islands of Greece in the Aegean Sea are there very accurately charted, but the expanded shorelines of those accurately located islands, and the presence of islands on the map which are now submerged, show that this portion of the Ibn Zara Map was transcribed from an ancient map of the Greek Aegean area that was obviously charted during the Ice Age, when the sea level was about 100 feet lower in that region of the world.

The remainder of this Ibn Zara Map of the Mediterranean (and Aegean) was compiled from other small precession-derived ancient source maps from Alexandria, but these source maps were apparently drawn after 1500 B.C., as the shorelines on the Ibn Zara Map (except of the Aegean portion) are also located with the noted great precision of the ancient mapmakers, but these shorelines are post-Ice Age, from when sea level had risen about 100 feet along Europe (relatively near where was the Ice Age ice-pack overburden).[4]

The location accuracies of the points of the shorelines on this map are far greater than those accuracies which were achieved with medieval expertise. The Turkish admirals could measure north to south distances by the position of the sun on the horizon, or by measurements of the angle of the Polestar to the horizon, but they only crudely estimated east-west distances by travel times, macro-geographical estimations, and crude geographically-relative timings of eclipses, because they did not have the precession-measuring and the therewith earth-measuring expertise which had been mastered by the ancient sea kings, but which was seemingly lost during the Dark Ages after the fall of Rome.

Since the accuracies on the Ibn Zara Map are far superior to medieval expertise, and so therefore, since this accurate map is plainly a compilation of ancient maps from Alexandria, it is obvious that one of the small source maps was drawn during the Ice Age (of the Aegean portion of the map), and the rest were drawn after 1500 B.C., when the sea level had risen.

Two map compilations of ancient source maps, in addition to the previously noted Oronteus Finaeus and Piri Reis Maps, also mysteriously locate and precisely chart Antarctica. And remember, according to orthodox academicians, Antarctica was not discovered until 1818 A.D. by the Russians, but because the Oronteus Finaeus Map of 1532 A.D., and the Piri Reis Map of 1513, along with the Buache and the Mercator Maps of the 1700's A.D., have charted with great accuracy the location and shorelines of Antarctica, it is obvious the Russians were not the first ones there, and to say that all of these mapmakers were just lucky is to be disingenuous, to say the least.

Mercator was the greatest cartographer of his day, and he produced several maps showing Antarctica (although it wasn't "discovered" 'til a hundred years later), and he also included the Oronteus Fineaus Map in his atlas of maps, so the greatest of mapmakers of relatively recent times accepted the validity of the source maps for his maps, but modern orthodox academicians "see nothing here."

Please note the pattern, mainstream scientists act as if the submerged megaliths don't exist, and they don't realize the advanced mapmaking and surveying capabilities of the ancients, so they can say that the medieval mapmakers just got lucky about Antarctica, and that the accuracies for the locations of the landmasses and their shorelines are merely fortuitous guesswork, but such does not explain away the all too apparent.

The Buache Map from the 1700's A.D. shows the two landmasses of Antarctica which are beneath the currently two-mile-deep overburden of snow and ice.[5] The accuracy of the outlines of the two huge islands was not confirmed until modern times with remote sensing devices which measure through 10,000 feet of snow and ice, therefore, it is evident that the ancients were sailing and mapping the globe with great accuracy, thousands of years ago, when the Ice Age was in its early stages. And the medieval mapmakers realized the ancients' mastery of cartography, so they rationally and happily utilized the ancients' superior workmanship to greatly further the Renaissance knowledge about world geography and cartography. In fact, it is rumored that Columbus had one of these maps to convince the royals to finance his voyage to the Americas.

Here then we have noted ancient precession-derived maps from the Phoenician sea kings, which show shorelines early in the Ice Age, shorelines during its peak, and shorelines after the Ice Age, so it does seem that the most ancient advanced building and navigating civilizations sprang-up suddenly, near the time of the beginning of the Ice Age, and flourished until even a bit after the Ice Age, as the climate dramatically changed, and legendary mass-migrations of tribes and kingdoms were forced by that changing climate, and by the risensea level.

The actual cause of the Ice Age, which is not understood by most mainstream scientists, renders realistic these evidences for this unorthodox timeline for the beginning and ending of the Ice Age, and we will explore the true cause of the Ice Age which fulfilled the hydrological requirements for such a blitz of snow in the more extreme latitudes, and such heavy rain in the middle latitudes. The Ice Age did not last for hundreds of thousands of years, as indicated with this ancient cartographical evidence.

And as the true cause for the Ice Age precludes its having had lasted for more than 1,000 years, the scientific parameters for the Ice Age, which ended circa 1500 B.C., fit the time-period evidenced with the accurate ancient cartography from the Tyranean Sea Fish of Phoenicia, and those parameters, to be analyzed, fit the date of when the Great Pyramid was built, with its astronomically-derived dimensions, that was the base geographical reference point and distance standard for the accurate precession mapping by the ancients, during the Ice Age.

The great Chinese geographer Chang Heng was producing maps of unprecedented accuracies around 100 A.D., and it was said that for his mapmaking he had "cast a network of coordinates about heaven and earth, and reckoned on the basis of it." The title of one of his lost books about cartography was *Discourse on Net Calculations*, and he also produced his Birds-Eye Map, so these conjure-up thoughts about the "birds-eye-views" of observers looking directly down upon the established reference points of the medieval precession-based maps, sourced from ancient maps, with projections of distances to geographical points radially emanating from these reference points, and so, a net of the lines chris-crossed as they emanated radially from their respective reference points, and that gives the appearance of a net.

Such notions concerning birds-eye views and networks of coordinates about heaven and earth with which to reckon bring us back to the precession-derived dimensions of the Great Pyramid of Giza. The ancients had begun to chart "networks of coordinates about the heaven and the earth" when they "reckoned" where on the earth's surface after 4,320 years (one side of earth hexagon, 60 degrees x 72 years/degree) would the then observed position of the constellations on the horizon appear the same because of the precession of the earth's axis which manifests as the apparent slow movement of constellations along the horizon.

They reckoned distances with the archaeometer by measuring "networks of coordinates about the heaven and the earth" in relationship to the rate of the precession of the earth's axis, which manifests as a slow movement of the constellations along the horizon, that would rotate one full circle in 25,920 years, and therefore, the constellations appear to move along the horizon at the rate of 1 degree per 72 years (see Appendix I).

Another famous Chinese cartographer from around 200 A.D. was Phei Hsiu, who wrote in the preface to his Atlas that:

> *The origin of maps and geographical treatises goes far back into former ages. Under the three dynasties Hsia, Shang, and Chou (2000 B.C. to 1000 B.C.) there were special officials (Kuo Shih) for this. Then when the Han people sacked Hsien-yang, Hsiao Ho collected all the maps and documents of the Chin. Now it is no longer possible to find the old maps in secret archives, and even those which Hsiao Ho found are missing, we have only maps, both general and local, from the later Han time. None of these employs a graduated scale (fen lu) and none of them is arranged in a rectangular grid.*[6]

As a side-note, the rectangular grids were applied to the ancient source maps of precession-derived distances and directions of geographical locations for convenience sake. The points for the grid system were established with archaeometer-measured precession data, and then the gridding was applied as the earliest form of the recording of selected latitudes and longitudes for efficient communication of geographical coordinates. Some of the Turkish maps show the radial lines of the precession-measured geography, and they also show the latitude/longitude grid which was applied for expedience.

Another anomalously accurate medieval map called the Hua I Thu (which means Map of China and the Barbarian Countries) was carved into stone in 1137 A.D., and it is now kept in the Forest of Stelas in Xian China. This map accurately shows the rivers of China and their tributaries with location accuracies that would not be matched (like the ancient map-sourced medieval Turkish maps) until modern times, and therefore, not surprisingly, this map was also reputed to have been a compilation of ancient source maps.

The accuracies of the courses of China's rivers and their tributaries on this stone-map belie all medieval earth-measuring skills, so it is apparent that the source maps for the Hua I Thu were indeed produced by ancient ancestors from around 2000 B.C., during the Hsia dynasty, as also was the case with the mapmaking by the great Chinese cartographers Chang Heng and Phei Hsiu, from near the time of Christ.

The accurately located courses of China's rivers and streams on the Hua I Thu Map virtually match those on modern maps, but the rivers which flow into the Yellow Sea of eastern China extend farther on the Hua I Thu Map, because they enter a much smaller Yellow Sea on that map which shows the lower shoreline of the Yellow Sea during the Ice Age that is confirmed with computer-generated simulation maps of the Ice Age sea level in that region.

I urge you to access the book *Maps of the Ancient Sea Kings* by Charles Hapgood (with a Note therein written by no less than Albert Einstein), which provides pictures of all these anomalously accurate medieval maps, showing coastlines of the landmasses as they were during the Ice Age, when sea level was a few hundred feet lower than today, and so, when roughly 25 million square miles of now shallow seafloor were dry land, upon which megaliths of astronomical-measuring significance from circa 2000 B.C. were constructed by the ancient navigators who settled and charted these regions.

4

CHAPTER

Ancient Legends Reveal Precession

Certain same base 6 denominated numbers such as 12, 36, 54, 72, 108, 144, and 432, are integral to the legends of various ancient civilizations from all over the globe. These shared legendary numbers reveal the ancients' quantification with the archaeometer of the slow wobble of the earth's axis that causes locations of constellations on the horizon from year to year to apparently move slowly along at the rate of 72 years per 1 degree out of 360 degrees.

The Hindus of India say that earth history is divided into yugas of time which are multiples of 432,000 years, and each yuga of time began after a global catastrophe, sometimes caused by water, and sometimes by fire, which are called pralayas. The Hindu religion was founded by the ancient people of the Indus/Sarasvati and Tamil civilizations, who passed-down their knowledge through the Vedic literature, which is the backbone of Hinduism.

The number 432, utilized to denominate these periods of time called yugas, evidently came from the knowledge of precession mapping, because 432 is the precession-derived number denomination for the circumference of the earth, which was derived by the Egyptians when they masterminded the dimensions of the Great Pyramid of Giza. That monument of precession mapping which was the ancient global mapping base-location is a 1/43,200th scale model of a pyramid which would fit within the earth, with its base-corners touching the equator, and with its apex touching the North Pole.

Did the ancient Tamil and Indus civilizations, a few thousand miles to the east of Giza, who passed-down the legends of the Vedic literature for Hinduism, select this number for any particular reason? Why this number 432? Why not 423, or 324, or 243? We have seen that the ancients were navigating and settling the globe with precession-measured maps during the Ice Age, and some of those settlers built the Tamil/Kumari Kandam and Indus/Sarasvati civilizations, so it quite obvious that the number 432 was gleaned from precession-mapping knowledge, and not plucked out of thin air.

And according to Norse legend, the terrible last battle between the gods of order of Valhalla and the gods of disorder, symbolized by the Wolf, will culminate with the forces of Valhalla ruling the day, and then ruling the rest of eternity. To achieve this eternal victory, it was said that for the great battle:

> *500 doors and 40 there are I ween,*
> *in Valhalla's walls; 800 fighters through*
> *each door fare,*
> *When to war with the Wolf they go.*[1]

Let's see, a total of 540 doors times 800 fighters equals that ubiquitous precession number 432,000, just like the Hindu yugas of time, and as apparently from the 1/43,200th scale-down of the earths dimensions which are the dimensions of the Great Pyramid of Giza. Call it coincidence, but the evidence will continue to mount that coincidence could not have played into all of this.

Note that 540 also is a base 6 precession-derived number, and it is representative of 1½ times around the circle of the earth, as 360 degrees plus 180 degrees equals the 540 figure. The number of doors in Valhalla's walls could have just as easily been the precession number 720, with 600 fighters proceding from each door, for the total again of 432,000.

The ancient megalithic ruins of immense and precisely-hewn

blocks at Baalbeck in Lebanon near the coast of the Mediterranean include the ruins of 54 columns[2] which surrounded the Canaanite ancient temple for the worship of the sun god Baal. And according to Egyptian tradition, the wooden coffin of the mythological god-king Osiris floated from Egypt to Baalbeck, after the 72 conspirators against him had done their dirty deed.[3]

The death of Osiris symbolized the setting, and thereby temporary death, of the sun, and as it seems to circle the 360 degrees of the earth to rise each morning in a mythologically rejuvenated state, it is not surprising that 72 conspirators from the same forces of disorder of the Norse Valhalla legend would attempt to eternally do away with the supposed forces of order, led by the sun (Osiris), along with the other stars, which orderly seem to course through the heavens.

The 72 conspirators times 360 degrees of the circle of the earth equals 25,920 years for one cycle of the precession of the earth's axis that manifests as the slow apparent movement of the constellations' locations from year to year along the horizon, which was measured with the archaeometer, and was incorporated for the surveying, mapmaking, and timekeeping system of the ancients that is the root of our modern system. So why were there 72 conspirators if not from precession-measurements? Why not 70, or 75?

With the archaeometer, the ancients measured the rate at which constellations' locations on the horizon through the years seem to move along the horizon at a rate of 72 degrees per 1 degree of 360 degrees, so thereafter, the various tribes and nations who were aware of the measurement of the earth by this precession rate decided to incorporate these precession-derived numbers into their cryptic tales about the actions of their gods in relationship to the earth and cosmos.

At the ancient palace ruins of Apadana of the ancient Elamites in Iran are the remains of 72 columns which surround the palace ruins,[4] and there are 72 bell-shaped stupas which comprise the famous temple in Java of Borobudur.[5] In the proto-Hindu Indus region of northwest India at Dwarka is the previously discussed ancient temple, which happens to have 72 columns.[6]

The Rig Veda of these ancient Hindus tells of "the 12-spoked wheel in which 720 sons of Agni are established."[7] With 720 we have numbered 1/2 degrees of a full circle (as 2 x 360 = 720), which when multiplied by the 12 constellations of the zodiac, gives us the number 8,640, which is exactly twice the number 4,320 of years that it takes for the constellations to move along one side of the earth hexagon because of the slow wobble of the earth's axis, like a gyroscope in space that would wobble through one full cycle in 25,920 years.

So the constellations move 3,600 nautical miles (or 7,200 Great Pyramid base-perimeter lengths) along one side of the earth hexagon in 4,320 years, and therefore, as our timekeeping units are base 6 subdivisions (seconds, minutes, hours) of a 360 day year, it follows that our timekeeping system it based upon precession, because the same numbers for both time and distance are by the design figured from precession.

Notice that 86,400 is the number of seconds in a day, and so, we can see the linkage of the ancient precession mapping to our timekeeping system. The 86,400 seconds in a day when divided by 24 hours/day gives us 3,600 seconds per hour, and 3,600 is 1/2 the number 7,200 which was used by the ancients to subdivide one side of the earth hexagon to establish the perimeter-length for the base of the Great Pyramid, so we can see that our timekeeping system derives from the ancients' measurements of the slow movement of the constellations like a merry-go-round the horizon, this is the "wheel of time."

Do you see the connection? Time and distance were related by the ancients with the measurements from the archaeometer, as they equated the rate (distance divided by time) that the constellations move along the horizon with the amount of time that it would take the constellations to move 1/6th of the way around the 360 degree circle of the earth. And as they calculated 4,320 years for the constellations to move along one side of the earth hexagon, they knew that the distance covered in 4,320 years represents the radius length of the earth, because the length of one side of a hexagon (a six-sided polygon) is the same length as is the radius of the circle of the earth which circumscribes said hexagon.

The ancient Hung League of China has a precession-number

communication system whereby they engage in oral traditions of dialogue with the numbers of the subject material being denominated in precession numbers like the monetary quantities of 18, 36, 72, 108, 360, 720, etc., and these same precession numbers are integral to their ancient ritual dialogues for initiation.[7] We noted the ancient precession-measuring knowledge which is reflected in the maps of the ancient Chinese, so these Hung League traditions were apparently passed-down from those Ice Age precession-navigators.

As the Ice Age mariners were sailing and mapping much of the world around 2000 B.C., it is not surprising that the precession numbers are also prevalent within the traditions and astronomical methodologies of the Mayans of Central America. For their ancient solar calendar, a Tun is 360 days, a Katun is 7,200 days, and a Baktun is 144,000 days,[8] so if the Mayan calendar is not also derived from the precession mapping by their earliest ancestors who were sailing the high seas during the Ice Age, then that would defy all the odds, and that would buck the prevalence of precession numbers inherent to the traditions of many of the other ancient civilizations from around the world.

5

CHAPTER

Ice Age Rain for the Ancients

This world was navigated and charted during and after the Ice Age by seafarers who where privy to the results of the brainstorming for the design and dimensions of the Great Pyramid of Giza. The surveying for the Great Pyramid was conducted through precession measurements with the archaeometer, and those same precession measurements were utilized to "reckon networks of coordinates of the heaven and the earth" by the ancient Chinese cartographers.

Equipped with the archaeometer and seaworthy vessels like the twelve high-prowed, sixty to well over one-hundred foot long wooden vessels, which were found buried in the sands of Egypt, just west of the Giza Pyramid complex, they moved out onto the open seas with confidence, as with the archaeometer, they could measure where on earth they were in relationship to the earth-measuring geographical base reference point which was the Great Pyramid of Giza.

One vessel found buried in the sand next to the Great Pyramid is a one-hundred forty foot long, high-prowed and wooden-planked vessel, which according to the wear on the hull, keel, and gangway, had been much used at sea,[1] and was eventually buried in a funerary rite, so that the pharaohs of Egypt could assume their place in the afterlife as stars ("got to be a star") and ride across the sky in their celestial boats which are symbolized with the buried seagoing vessels.[2]

The high-prowed open-boat design of these buried Egyptian vessels are strikingly similar to the traditional designs of the reed-composed vessels seen on the Nile, at Lake Titicaca in Bolivia, and in the delta of the Euphrates in Mesopotamia. And the design is remarkably similar to the high-prowed wooden vessels of those great Viking navigators, so it seems that the precession mapping and navigation of much of the world by the Ice Age mariners was performed in vessels like those buried at Giza, and those vessels are memorialized with that traditional boat design in various parts of the world today.

When the Great Pyramid was being constructed during the Ice Age, when those ancients were also mapping and navigating the globe, and when they were beginning to build the great megalithic cultures whose ruins (both onshore and submerged) are found all over the world, the climate and ecology of the earth was very different than today. With the intense snow-blitz in the more extreme latitudes during the Ice Age came also much more rainfall than today in the middle latitudes.

The Sahara Desert was then a patchwork of lakes and rivers that supported subtropical flora and fauna, and the current desert of eastern Pakistan and northwest India was then also a grassy and forested land, with the now dried-up Sarasvati River memorialized in the Vedic literature as having been a big vital river-drainage system for the then thriving Indus-Sarasvati civilization.

And the present desolate desert wilderness of the Middle East was also then prairies of grasslands and rolling forested hills, which all supported teeming wildlife, provided abundant building materials, and were indicative of the amounts of rainfall which were required for the agricultural needs of those ancient civilizations with their hundreds of thousands of people who evidently inhabited those regions during the Ice Age.

The Sahel is a name for the Sahara Desert region of northern Africa, and Sahel translates from the ancient Arab word for shoreline, which refers to the inter-connected lakes and rivers during the Ice Age that are now a dried-up series of evaporite-encrusted basins which stretch the length and breadth of the Sahara Desert.

On the northern shore of one of these now dried-up lakes (about two-hundred miles west of the Giza Plateau) is the natural spring and now oasis of Siwa, which is the site of the Nabta megalithic ruins that was first developed when it was on the shoreline of this lake during the Ice Age. Siwa was a sacred city to the ancient Egyptians, and it is extensively referred to in the ancient Egyptian texts.

The megalithic ruins there include stone-circles of huge vertical slabs of rock with astronomical-measuring significance which reflect the ancient knowledge about the equinoxes and solstices,[3] and may have reflected a knowledge of earth precession in relationship to the constellations, as is reflected at Stonehenge in England (I say may have reflected that knowledge because of the ruined state of the stone-circles of Nabta).

Etchings on rocks in the area depicting crocodiles, gazelles, cattle, and men fishing the marshy shorelines of these ancient inland lakes of the Sahara, show that the megalithic builders on the shorelines of these now dried-up lakes subsisted on the indigenous wildlife which thrived around and along those lakes and interconnecting rivers, which were fed by the generous rainfall there during the Ice Age.[4]

Lake Chad, in a basin on the southern edge of the Sahel, was many times larger during the Ice Age, as reflected by lake deposits on the hills in the area, but it remains today in its greatly diminished state because sufficient water flows into it by the rivers which originate in the highlands to the south of central Africa. The other basins of the Sahara are not the recipients of sufficient river-inflows from highlands, so they have dried-up, leaving behind the tell-tale sediments which were deposited on the lakes' bottoms before the lakes had dried-up, within a few centuries after the circa 1500 B.C. end of the Ice Age.

There are mountain ranges smack-dab in the middle of the Sahara, but it is so dry there that no water is retained in the soil to flow out and down as artesian springs to merge as streams. During the Ice Age, these mountains were the high-ground surrounded by the basin lakes of the Sahara, and at a low elevation on the Ahaggar Mountains of southern Algeria are evidences of a megalithic boat dock for maritime commerce,[5] and rock etchings in the area also depict the flora and fauna of the abundant subtropical environment there in the Sahel (which means shoreline) during the Ice Age.

In the Nubian desert south of Egypt on the eastern shorelines of the Ice Age Sahel flourished the ancient Nubian kingdom which was a constant nemesis to the ancient Egyptians. Many pyramids similar to those of ancient Egypt dot the landscape in that now parched and desolate part of the world, and with those pyramids are found more stone-circles of astronomical-measuring function.[6]

Were these pyramid-building and astronomy-measuring settlers there so bold (or so masochistic) as to develop their culture in a parched and desolate desert at the time when stone-circles and other megalithic structures are said by mainstream archaeologists to have begun to be built circa 2000 B.C.? Remember, mainstream scientists stubbornly adhere to the notion that the Ice Age ended previously by 8,000 years, when they say that the lush, well-watered, and Ice-Age-caused environments in the middle latitudes of the world turned to dust.

Ancient Mesopotamia, known as the Cradle of Civilization, is peppered with ancient ziggarauts (pyramids) of the Sumerians (Babylonians) that were built of bricks made from the local clay of the Tigris and Euphrates river valleys. They apparently saw no need to inconveniently venture faraway to secure limestone or granite blocks with which to build their sacred pyramids dedicated to their gods of the starry heavens.

And yet, mainstream archaeologists would have us believe that yes, they did build their pyramids with locally available materials, but that no, they did not also harvest their lumber, wildlife, and wild-vegetables for their hundreds of thousands of people from what was locally available, because that region was a desert, according to mainstream archaeologists and climatologists, when the clay-brick pyramids were being constructed circa 2000 B.C. Therefore, we are supposed to believe that the ancient Sumerians settled on admittedly two fine waterways (the Tigris and Euphrates rivers) which sluiced through a parched and treeless wilderness, and therefore, with nothing but the rivers for their sustenance, amid seas of sand on either side of the rivers.

In fact, how the other ancient kingdoms of that region circa 2000 B.C., such as of Elam (where is Susa), of the Amorites (west of Babylon), and of the Gutis (north of Babylon, who became the Goths[7]), and also of the Egyptians, could have flourished with their hundreds of thousands of people in that supposedly then virtually rainless region of the globe defies credulity. Are we to think that they traveled hundreds of miles for their wood? And where are the vast networks of canals for field irrigation which would be required to support many thousands of people in their city-states of relatively small areas? And where were the grasslands to feed their thousands of head of livestock? Did they haul grass from hundreds of miles away?

Mainstream scientists concur that during the Ice Age, the Middle East was a land of rolling hills, with forests and plains of grasslands, and fruit trees surrounding the now dried-up lakes and streams which are evidenced (as also in the Sahara) through surface geological studies of these now desert regions. But they say that these lush environments turned to dust 8,000 years before the first great megalithic builders decided to develop the land in a supposedly then desert environment at around 2000 B.C. Does that make sense to you?

Orthodox archaeologists would never admit that the Ice Age actually ended at around 1500 B.C., so they thereby are indirectly admitting that the Middle East and Egypt were deserts at the time when the advanced megalithic building cultures of Sumer (Babylonia) and Egyptian sprang-up suddenly, because actually, with the Ice Age came the heavy rains in the middle latitudes from the dense cloud-cover which then necessarily encompassed the whole world, and so, provided that plentiful rainfall in the Middle East and Egypt.

The same can be said of the now parched and desolate Indus-Sarasvati region of northwest India and eastern Pakistan, where were built extensive cities of clay-brick buildings of the Indus-Sarasvati civilization, complete with gridded systems of streets and sanitation plumbing, both on land and on the now submerged seafloor because of the prodigious sea level rise which was caused by the melting of thousands of vertical feet of Ice Age icepack. These structures are of designs and functions commonly attributed to 2000 B.C., but mainstream scientists turn a blind-eye to these submerged structures, and then they can, through their obfuscation, say that the structures onshore are of 2000 B.C. vintage.

But somewhat unorthodox archaeologists like Graham Hancock and a few Indian scientists such as B.R. Rao have noted the validity of the evidence from sonar scans and salvaged relics from the submerged Indus civilization cities.[8] The recovered relics are tools and jewelry which are characteristic of the Indus-Sarasvati civilization, acknowledged by almost all to have flourished circa 2000 B.C., not circa 10000 B.C., as Hancock would have us believe.

About one-hundred miles inland from the seashore in the parched wilderness of extreme northwestern India is the ancient river-port city of Lothal, complete with loading docks and ship maintenance quays.[9] This inland port was on the now dried-up Sarasvati River which then flowed down from the western Himalayan foothills and emptied into the present Gulf of Kutch during the Ice Age. Here we have an acknowledged Indus Civilization river-port city of circa 2000 B.C., now in the middle of the desert, which was built along the now-dried-up Sarasvati River, which mainstream scientists say dried-up when they say the Ice Age ended at around 10000 B.C.

Do you see the contradiction? We are dealing with a river-port city from 2000 B.C. that was on a river which supposedly dried-up about 8,000 years before the commonly acknowledged date for the river-port city's heyday, so why are mainstream scientists allowed to get away with such blatant evidentiary hypocrisy? It is because these Ice Age archaeological contradictions are swept under the rug to maintain the orthodox status quo. Orthodox academicians say "look, we are the experts here, trust us, we know what we are doing," and so then, the public generally trusts the dogma of these ivory tower elitists because, by and large, the public is ignorant of the issues.

With this Indus civilization river-port city of Lothal (now in the middle of a river-free desert), one could not ask for a more fool-proof evidence that the Ice Age actually ended after 2000 B.C. After all, this city and the many others, like Harappa and Mohenjo-Daro, in that now desert region of eastern Pakistan and northwest India, are said to have flourished circa 2000 B.C., and remember too that the submerged megaliths just offshore from Dwarka and in the Gulfs of Cambay and Kutch are of forms and functions indicative that they were built around 2000 B.C., and then they were submerged when the Ice Age ended.

This evidence would force orthodox archaeologists to say that the ancient river-port city of Lothal and the other ancient cities actually flourished there on the Ice Age Sarasvati River drainage-system at the popularly held 10000 B.C. date for the end of the Ice Age, but such would defy their consensus that the Indus civilization flourished circa 2000 B.C., and thusly, they would then abide with Hancock in a position which also contradicts the evidence, if only the public would hold their feet to the fire for an explanation about this obvious archaeological enigma.

The ancient Hindu text Rig Veda which is thought to have been commentary from around 2000 B.C. says:

> *Coming together, glorious, loudly roaring-Sarasvati, Mother of Floods...with fair streams flowing, full swelling with the volume of their water...*[10]
>
> *She with her might...hath burst with strong waves the ridges of the hills...Yea, the divine Sarasvati, terrible with her golden path, foe-slayer...whose limitless unbroken flood, swift-moving with a rapid rush, comes onward with tempestuous roar...Yea, she most dear amidst dear streams...graciously inclined, Sarasvati hath earned our praise.*[11]

Here is an ancient Indian literary description from circa 2000 B.C. of this once mighty ancient river whose river channel is confirmed by the surface geology and satellite photos, which has remaining next to it the ancient Indus-Sarasvati civilization river-port city of

Lothal, thought to have flourished around 2000 B.C.

If the orthodox notion that the Ice Age really ended at around 10000 B.C. were valid, then these ancient literary descriptions of the once roaring Sarasvati River would necessarily have also been from 10000 B.C., when quasi-cavemen were supposedly just figuring-out farming and tool-making, and so, when sophisticated language such as the descriptive prose noted above from the Hindu Rig Veda is considered to have been highly unlikely. And note again that the Hindu scholars say that those stories about the Sarasvati are from around 2000 B.C.

The abundant rainfall during the Ice Age, which caused the lush vegetation to burst forth for these ancient civilizations of Egypt, Babylon, and the Indus-Sarasvati, also caused much rain erosion on the limestone megaliths of ancient Egypt. The Great Sphinx, just east of the Great Pyramid, both on the west side of the Nile, was sculpted by quarrying out the surrounding limestone strata, so the Sphinx sits within a quarry pit. And the limestone walls of this quarry pit show deep vertical erosion gullies which are characteristic of heavy water erosion from heavy rainfall.[12]

Dr. Robert Schoch of Boston University has kicked-up a lot of dust within the scientific community by noting that such erosion should never have occurred in the ancient Egypt imagined by orthodox archaeologists, which must have been quite arid at around 2000 B.C., because they say that the Ice Age, with its heavy rains in the middle latitudes, ended circa 10000 B.C.

Hancock and Schoch propose that, therefore, the megalithic building in ancient Egypt actually dates back to perhaps around 10000 B.C., so the ivory tower types are all up-in-arms because the plain evidence of heavy water erosion, due to heavy rainfall in the limestone quarry, is an enigma which they cannot explain away. How can they explain heavy rain erosion from around 2000 B.C. with their climate chronology?

As Hancock says in regard to this seemingly anomalous rain-caused limestone erosion, as it relates to the mainstream timeline for ancient Egypt:

> *Does this not suggest that the climate could have been very different when the Sphinx enclosure was carved-out? What would have been the sense of creating this immense statue if its destiny were merely to be engulfed by the shifting sands of the eastern Sahara? However, since the Sahara is a young desert, and since the Giza area in particular was wet and relatively fertile 11,000 to 15,000 years ago, is it not worth considering another scenario altogether? Is it not possible that the Sphinx enclosure was carved out during those distant green millennia when topsoil was still anchored to the surface of the plateau by the roots of grasses and shrubs, and when what is now a desert of windblown sand more closely the rolling savannahs of modern Kenya and Tanzania?*[13]

The megalithic limestone blocks which compose the so-called Valley Temple, which is fifty feet south of the Sphinx,[14] also show supposedly anomalous evidence of heavy rain-erosion which the orthodox types would never have predicted with their idea that the heavy rains of the Ice Age ended at around 10000 B.C., which is about eight thousand years before when they think these megalithic structures were built. The limestone megalithic blocks of the Osireon at Abydos farther up the Nile also show this rainfall erosion from the rains of the Ice Age.

Please note that the timeline for the ancient Egyptian pharaohs, which is gospel to orthodox archaeologists, and which was written by the Egyptian historian Manetho circa 300 B.C., has mistakenly listed some of the pharaohs sequentially, who actually ruled contemporaneously in the various city-states (like Abydos, On, Memphis, etc.), and so, his chronology must be shortened from dating back to circa 3000 B.C., and it then fits the 2000 B.C. timeframe. Additionally, Egyptian regents (but not true pharaohs) were also listed by Manetho, therefore, the circa 3000 B.C. date for the earliest pharaohs is an exaggeration which orthodox archaeologists expediently overlook.

An also mistakenly trusted kings list, from the Babylonian historian Berosus of circa 300 B.C., dates the earliest Sumerian (Babylonian) kings also to circa 3000 B.C., but some of the kings included therewith were actually contemporaneous city-state rulers of Uruk, Akkad, Sippar, Nimrud, etc., who were mistakenly included sequentially, and so, the true chronology of the Babylonian kings also fits back to about 2000 B.C.

Notwithstanding the exaggerated length of these kings lists, watch for mainstream academicians to stretch the timeline for ancient Egypt, Babylon, and the Indus even farther back in time to about 7000 B.C., and look for them to move up their date for the end of the Ice Age to around 6000 B.C., so that they then can attempt to overlap their timeframe for the building of the megalithic structures with their timeframe for the end of the Ice Age, and so, attempt to rationalize the submerged megalithic ruins.

Hancock has already been working on moving-up the timeframe for the end of the Ice Age to around 6000 B.C., despite the fact that orthodox scientists say that most of the sea level rise caused by the melting of the Ice Age ice-pack occurred before 10000 B.C. (between 15000 and 10000 B.C.), as he admits with his just noted statement. He is trying to fit his square peg into the round hole.

And as the submerged megaliths off the coasts of the Indus, Egypt, China, and Japan are more and more exposed to public awareness, much through Hancock's popular books, and as the significance of those megalithic structures' presences on the seafloor vis-à-vis the time of end of the Ice Age becomes more and more apparent to the public, then the ivory tower types will be forced to move back their circa 2000 to 3000 B.C. date for the start of megalithic building, way back to around 7000 B.C., to expediently overlap Hancock's hoped-for revision of the date for the end of the Ice Age, way up to circa 6000 B.C. Here they will cooperatively attempt to fit the square peg into the round hole.

6
CHAPTER

Ancient Allegories for Precession

In the legends of various ancient cultures are allusions to the now popularly dubbed "wheel of time," that are actually ancestral allegories for the slow precession of the earth's axis, which manifests as the slow apparent movement of the constellations of the zodiac along the horizon at the rate of 72 years per 1 degree (of 360 degrees).

Obvious is the fact that the ancients were aware of precession, because their legends are replete with precession numbers which are directly attributable to ancient measurements with the archaeometer, so it is predictable that the ancients would also allegorically refer to this precession phenomenon as a sort of wheel of time in their legends about the nature of the cosmos, and of time itself.

The 12 spokes of the wheel of Agni from Hindu lore, analyzed in Chapter 4, represent the 12 constellations of the zodiac which seem to move clockwise slowly along the horizon like a wheel. And the 720 sons of Agni are symbolic of the 72 years/degree rate at which these constellations seem to move like a wheel around the horizon, so here we have the "wheel of time," which is actually the apparent movement of the constellations due to the slow wobble of the earth's axis, which would wobble once in 25,920 years.

This god Agni, known as the "light of the world," and who is the Hindu fire god, is therefore apparently the sun god, because that fiery ball in the sky lights up the world, as it provides daytime out of night, while the earth spins once in 24 hours. When 24 is divided into the 720 sons of Agni, the result is 30, which is the number of degrees out of 360 degrees that is the extent of the respective zodiac constellations on the circular horizon at dawn, because 360 degrees divided by 12 zodiac constellations (the 12 spokes of Agni's wheel) equals 30 degrees/constellation.

This sun god Agni rises in the morning with a new constellation appearing behind it every 30 days, because as this tilted earth orbits in its annual trip around the sun to cause the seasons, it also causes the constellations to seem to move clockwise along the horizon, and thereby, a new constellation gradually moves into position behind the dawn sun every 30 days, and hence we have the zodiac signs denoting peoples' birth dates.

But one cycle of the wobble of the axis of the earth (through 25,920 years) causes the constellation, which appears behind the dawn sun on a given date of the year, to seem to move the other way in a counter-clockwise circle around the horizon at the rate of 72 years/degree, and so, move away along the horizon from the dawn sun, and therefore, transition through 2,160 years to the next constellation of the zodiac to appear behind the dawn sun on a given date of the year.

This is the change from one zodiac age to the next zodiac age, for instance, as we are now at "the dawning of the age of Aquarius." The constellation of Aquarius is transitioning counter-clockwise, due to the precession-caused apparent movement of the constellations along the horizon, replacing the constellation of Pisces behind the dawn sun on the spring equinox (on a given date).

We need a specific date for precession measuring, because the sun appears on the horizon farther north in the summer, and farther south in winter (with the reverse in the southern hemisphere), therefore, in our current zodiacal age of Aquarius, the position of the constellations behind the rising sun changes through the year, from being housed in Sagittarius at the summer solstice, to Virgo at the autumn equinox, to Gemini at the winter solstice, and to now Aquarius at the spring equinox, as we are now at "the dawn of the new age of Aquarius," although some say that we have now been in the "new age" for a few decades already, and some say it won't happen until the year 2012, according to Mayan calculations.

So measurements of this slow counter-clockwise precession-caused apparent movement of the constellations along the horizon can effectively be measured from year to year with one same date used from year to year, like the date of the spring equinox, the preferred date by the ancients for precession-measuring reference, because that is when everything seems to come alive, like the rising sun seems to come alive at dawn.

The zodiac ages are 2,160 years long, because 12 constellations of the zodiac divided into 25,920 years for one cycle of the precession of the earth's axis equals 2,160 years. The zodiac constellations' apparent movement along the horizon for a new constellation to "house the sun" every 2,160 years is the transition through astronomical ages of time which the ancients allegorized as the wheel of time, like the 12 spokes of the wheel of Agni.

The determinative precession number 25,920 can be subdivided by any other precession number like 12, 36, 54, 72, or 108 to equal the precession numbers 2, 160, 720, 480, 360, and 240, so all of the precession-derived subdivisions of 25,920 will multiply-up, so to speak, with other precession-derived subdivisions of 25,920 to equal this ultimately determinative precession number, the number of years which it would take for the precession of the earth's axis to cycle one time.

So because the ancients have represented all of the subdivided precession numbers in their legends, calendars, or designs, it is obvious that the length of time required for the earth's axis to wobble once in space to cause the 12 constellations of the zodiac to appear to move once around the horizon was the standard for ancient timekeeping (and thereby accurate ancient mapping), and as herein discussed, it is the basis for our modern timekeeping and mapping system, because some of those same base 6 numbers of precession (24, 60, and 360) denominate our current system.

Two eminent orthodox academicians, science-history Professor Giorgio de Santillana of M.I.T. and Professor Hertha von Dechend of Frankfort University wrote a book in the sixties called *Hamlet's Mill*, which details the commonality of the precession numbers among the ancient cultures,[1] and Graham Hancock saw merit in their thesis, vis-à-vis the anomalously accurate ancient precession-derived maps, and so, he then elaborated upon their thesis with much more documentation of these precession numbers among the ancients, and he also linked Crichton Miller's patented archaeometer to the ancients' determination of the precession numbers, and so, Hancock made more robust this thesis that the ancients were measuring precession, and thereby, were accurately mapping much of the globe during the Ice Age.

The book title *Hamlet's Mill* refers to the ancient Icelandic legend (later co-opted by Shakespeare) which describes a celestial mill rotating around the axis of the earth. Santlillana and von Dechend refer to Hamlet's mill as "an orb (sphere) of heaven that turns like a millstone...," and remember that these same ancient Norsemen who made legend their spinning mill of time also displayed the knowledge of specific precession numbers, as seen in the legend of the 432,000 warriors of Valhalla which is noted in Chapter 4, so the ancient Norse ancestors were apparently also mapping and navigating the globe.

> *A great god of Hinduism is Vishnu, of whom it is said in the ancient book Rig Veda (from circa 2000 B.C.) that: "He like a rounded wheel, hath set in swift motion his 90 racing steeds together with the 4..."[2] And written a few verses previously in that Rig Veda, it is said that: "I will declare the mighty deeds of Vishnu, of him who measured out the earthly regions.[3]*

We shall later explore who may be this Vishnu (as ancient gods are often glorified ancestors), who could measure the earth, according to the plain statement which is corroborated with the other reference that Vishnu figuratively set in motion a base 6 number 90 of steeds, which when multiplied by the number 4 of basic directions, results in the precession number 360 of degrees that fill-out the circle of the earth, and that fill out of the circle of the rounded wheel of the constellations on the horizon, that is driven by the 90 steeds times 4 which pull this wheel, which thereby allowed Vishnu to measure the earth.

Remember that the ancient Indus-Sarasvati and Tamil/ Dravidian civilizations of India spawned these Vedic stories about the earliest ancestors of India, and remember that these ancient civilizations of India built megalithic structures which are oriented by astronomical measurements, and which demonstrate a knowledge of precession, as demonstrated with the 72 columns of the temple at Dwarka, and with the 72 columns of the temple at Apadana.

And because some of the Indus and Tamil megalithic structures are now on the seafloor, it is apparent that the Ice Age ended during the heyday of these Vedic cultures which are commonly acknowledged to have flourished circa 2000 B.C., and which have spawned the Vedic stories about measuring the earth and pushing a precession-referencing wheel of 90 steeds times 4 directions, which results in the number 360 of degrees which compose the circle of the earth, and which compose the circle along which the constellations appear to move across the horizon because of the slow wobble of the earth's axis.

The Vedic fire god Agni, who is also known as the light of the world, and so, is also the Vedic sun god who provides for the "Ag," as in agriculture of the world, and who is worshipped with fire altars, built by the ancient Indus and Tamil civilizations, which are composed of exactly 10,800 bricks,[4] a seemingly odd number, unless one is aware that 108 is a precession number common to many ancient legends and architectures. The number of verses in the ancient Rig Veda is exactly that same number 10,800, so all this is not because of the knowledge of precession, but is merely of coincidence and happenstance?

According to the legends of the precession-measuring ancients, the wheel of time, or the mill of time, or the whirlpool of time (as in Homer's maelstrom of the sea) is an allegory for the apparent movement of the constellations of the zodiac along the horizon through the centuries, and with a move into a new "house" for the sun, at dawn on the spring equinox, the ancients saw the cosmic drama of the zodiac being played out in the heavens, and so, saw this as being affective to the world, because when a new zodiac age was entered, global cataclysms were expected to be caused by the trauma which the cosmos supposedly endures when the sun enters its new house.

This notion of cosmic drama being played-out on earth carries through to this day, as many cultures are expecting a global cataclysm because the sun has entered its new Aquarius house, a supposed time of cosmic disorientation as the cosmos adjusts to this new housing for the sun. Let me point out however that when the zodiac age last changed about 2200 years ago, at around 200 B.C., no global geophysical calamities ensued, and as most all would agree that we entered the "age of Aquarius" around the year 2000 A.D., it seems that the "world tree" once again has not shaken on time.

Many people today lead their lives according to this movement of the patterns of the stars along the horizon, and such has been traditional since the time of the ancient precession-measurers, who saw the precession of the constellations along the horizon as being the very essence of time itself, and so, worshipped the sun and the slowly revolving constellations which were the actors in this imagined cosmic drama of the precession-driven cycles of time.

7

CHAPTER

CONSTANT TWILIGHT AND BLACK RAIN

The Mayans of Central America say that their ancient history books the *Chilam Baalam* and the *Popol Vuh* were passed down to them from their ancient ancestors who, according to the *Popol Vuh,* had sailed to their land from the east[1] during a time of black rain and constant twilight.[2] This *Popol Vuh* text also states that at that time, those ancients navigators "measured the round face of the earth and the arch of the sky."[3]

To the east, across the ocean from where the Mayan ancestors had navigated to their new land in Central America by measuring "the round face and the earth and the arch of the sky," rests the Great Pyramid of Egypt, the base reference point for ancient precession mapping, and the monument to the ancients' precession measurements with the archaeometer, as evidenced by the astronomically-derived dimensions of that Great Pyramid. Some historians have said that the Mayan Staff of Power may have been this archaeometer, also known as the Celtic Cross.

And that would not surprise me because ancient Mayan designations for periods of time are precession-derived numbers like 360 day tuns, 12,000 day baktuns, and 144,00 day katuns,[4] so this precession knowledge came from ancient ancestors who had navigated across the Atlantic with maps of precession-derived measurements like those which were utilized by Turkish Admiral Piri Reis to compile his map which very accurately charted the Atlantic, eastern South America, and even more amazingly, the Antarctic (see Chapter 3).

Near the eastern coastline of Central America are found huge upright megalithic head-statues, much like those on Easter Island in the Pacific, but these depict faces of African appearance, and are said to have been built by the Olmecs who later became the Toltecs, and then became the Mayans.[5] The Olmecs are commonly associated by orthodox archaeologists with the later Toltecs, and the Mayan tun, baktun, and katun precession periods of time are documented on Olmec rock engravings,[6] so here we see a cultural continuum from the Olmecs, through the Toltecs, to the Mayans.

Mainstream archaeologists would have us believe that almost if not all of the first settlers in the New World came across the Bering land-bridge during the Ice Age when sea level was much lower, and so, Alaska was then connected with Siberia. This is the orthodox position because they say that these first humans in the Americas came across about 30,000 years ago, which is some 25,000 years before they think that sailing the high seas was practicable.

They do concede that perhaps a few of the earliest settlers in the Americas may have bumped along the Ice Age coastline of the Bering Land Bridge in skin-covered wooden-ribbed tubs, wearing animal skin outfits and toting stone age tools. But there in Central America, we see the ancient Olmec statues with African looking features, and records in rock of Olmec precession numbers, which indicate sophisticated mapping and navigating by the Olmecs, not to mention the impressive Olmec step-pyramids found there, like at Palenque, Chichen Itza, Teotihuacan, La Venta and other locations on the Yucatan.

Of course, many ancients did come to the Americas via the Bering land-bridge during the Ice Age which ended circa 1500 B.C., but most of those naturally settled in western North America, and they seem to have not had the precession knowledge as did the great megalithic builders of Central and South America who had astronomically-oriented megalithic buildings, and in the case of the Olmec-descended Mayans, a calendar based upon precession measurements.

The *Popol Vuh* speaks of black rain and constant twilight when the Olmec ancestors sailed from their ancestral homeland in North Africa, and those conditions jibe with the rampant volcanic upheavals caused during the Ice Age by the isostatic vertical displacements of continental crust because of the increasingly huge overburden weight from the Ice Age icepack's build-up, and because of the isostatic rebound at the end of the Ice Age, when the two mile-deep Ice Age icepack melted and poured into the sea, to cause sea level to rise about 300 feet in the middle latitudes, and less than that nearer the continental landmasses on which the Ice Age icepack's overburden had rested.

The rampant volcanism of the Ice Age is evidenced by much volcanic ash within today's polar icecaps[7] that had fallen from the sky with the Ice Age snow-blitz in the extreme latitudes, and with the heavy rainfall in the middle latitudes, described in the *Popol Vuh* as black rain. And the black rain fell during a time of constant twilight, which is indicative of the dense worldwide cloud-cover necessary to produce the much heavier snowfalls and rainfalls during the Ice Age in the various parts of the world.

There is a ten-foot-diameter wheel-shaped megalithic structure with a round piece (the earth) in the center that is found at La Venta in southeastern Mexico of the ancient Olmec civilization. On the megalithic wheel are six equally-spaced dot-marks, which indicate the points of the hexagon of the circle of the earth,[8] if the points were hexagonally connected by lines within the wheel. And with the earth as the round stone in the middle, it seems that this megalithic wheel of the Olmecs portrays the hexagonal methodology which was utilized to quantify time by the measurement of the slow apparent movement of the constellations along the horizon, which is caused by the slow wobble of the earth's axis like a gyroscope in space.

The Mayans, who descended from the ancient Olmecs, have a precession-derived calendar system, and the Olmecs navigated from across the Atlantic to their new land with an apparent knowledge of precession measurements, as indicated with their hexagon-indicating wheel, and with their precession-derived number system, so these evidences are highly corroborative of North Africans having navigated across the Atlantic during the Ice Age in a time of black rain and constant twilight, as it was then, according to the ancient *Popol Vuh* of the Mayans.

The megalithic heads with features of Africans in the land of the Olmecs jibes with the gene pool of the modern population there of southeastern Mexico. A supposedly anomalous quantity of African genes (of the so-called Garifuna people) are within the population that reflects an African presence in Central America several millennia ago, and the DNA data does not indicate that these African genes are from the slave trade of relatively recent times,[9] so the African blood from several millennia ago dovetails with the presence of these supposed (by mainstream scientists) to be anomalous African head-statues of the Olmecs.

The Avesta writings of the ancient Aryans, who lived in western Russia during the early stages of the Ice Age, describe the devastating onset of snow and ice in the old home-country to the north when:

> *Ten months of winter are there now, two months of summer, and these are cold as to the water, cold as to the earth, cold as to the trees... There all around falls deep snow, that is the direst of plagues.*[10]

The account then describes how that because of this onslaught of snow and ice, the Aryans were forced to migrate south into the Middle East, and on into northwestern India, where they evidently challenged the hegemony of the Vedic people of the Indus civilization during the Ice Age circa 2000 B.C., when the great cities on the Indus and Sarasvati Rivers were thriving, and before the Ice Age ended to cause sea level to rise about 300 feet in that region, to engulf some of those cities which are now found far offshore on the shallow seafloor.

The ancient Toba tribe of the Gran Chaco region of the east-central slopes of the Andes Mountains in South America describe the legendary time of the Great Cold, when:

> *Asin told a man to gather as much wood as he could and to cover the hut with a thick layer of thatch because of time of great cold was coming. As soon as the hut had been prepared, Asin and the man shut themselves inside and waited. When the great cold set in, shivering people arrived to beg a firebrand from them. Asin was hard and gave embers only to those who had been his friends. The people were freezing, and the cried the whole night. At midnight they were all dead, young and old, men and women…this period of ice and sleet lasted for a long time and all the fires were put out. Frost was as thick as leather.*[11]

The ancient Tobas of the Andes experienced snow and ice during the Ice Age because of the relatively great elevation of the Gran Chaco region compared to the coastal plains on which the Olmecs settled in southeastern Mexico. As it rained mightily during the Ice Age in these middle latitudes, it also snowed at the higher elevations in those same middle latitudes, so the glaciers that we see in the Andes, the Himalayas, and the other high mountain ranges are mere remnants of Ice Age icepacks which then extended thousands more vertical feet down these mountain ranges.

The land of the famous Inca Empire of the Andes, with its awesome megalithic buildings and ceremonial edifices to the sun, was apparently at lower elevations during the Ice Age, because the huge overburden of the Ice Age icepack on the high Andes had pushed down the western portion of South America. Such is indicated with the ancient shorelines on the hills around Lake Titicaca that are not parallel to the current shoreline.[12] This shows that isostatic-rebound-uplift of the region occurred when the Ice Age icepack overburden had dissipated with the end of the Ice Age, when differential regional rebound-uplift caused the ancient shoreline to skew from the horizontal because some sections rebounded more than others.

The ancient megalithic port city on Lake Titicaca was Tiahuanaco, which is now five miles from the lake's now receded shoreline. The lake was at a higher level during the Ice Age, because of much more rain and snow in the those lower Andes. And in that area are found the flooded-out remains of urban life in the rocky debris, because when the Ice Age ended, water surged down from the high Andes and flooded out the megalithic city of Tiahuanaco, leaving behind the clear signs of massive flows of water which destroyed the city.

In the centuries following, the greatly reduced rainfall and snow, which made the area a desert, caused Lake Titicaca to recede to its current size, leaving the port city of huge megalithic-block walls and megalithic ceremonial plazas and columns, which were of the ancient port-city of Tiahuanaco, some five miles from the now receded shoreline. The area now is a desolate wasteland without vegetation, it looks like a moonscape, while during the Ice Age, it was rainy with lush vegetation.

And yet, orthodox archaeologists would have us believe that the advanced megalithic building, with giant sculpted stone blocks, that make-up the remains of the old port city Tiahuanaco, happened long after the Ice Age had ended, when that region would have been the treeless desert which it is today, and when the shoreline of Titicaca would have already receded miles from the megalithic docks and quays of Tiahuanaco, which therefore would have served no purpose.

So once again, we face a great enigma of ancient history, which is unavoidably the result of the proffer by mainstream archaeologists who are locked into their orthodox timeline, that the advanced megalithic builders of the Indus, Egypt, Sumer, Central America, and the Andes chose to develop their respective civilizations' megalithic-building sites in desert wastelands, about 8,000 years after those geographical areas had ceased to be well-watered and fertile grasslands and forests during the, proposed by the orthodox, time of the Ice Age, which ended at supposedly around 10000 B.C.

And how should we judge the timeframes for the legends

from the pre-Mayan book *Popol Vuh*, and from the ancient Toba tribe of the Andes, that vividly describe Ice Age conditions of black rain, constant twilight (because of the dense cloud-cover), and the onset of that long darkened period when men huddled in their abodes around the fire to escape the chilling precipitation which seemed to fall incessantly in the early days of those civilizations? Are these tribal recollections really from 10000 B.C., when mainstream scientists say that the Ice Age was in its final stages, which is 8,000 years before when those same scientists say that megalithic building began?

If so, then those Ice Age legends were successfully passed-down for 8,000 years until the time for the beginning of megalithic building at around 2000 B.C., with no accounts of other historical occurrences for those 8,000 years, which would logically be included in the ancentral recollections, if they are really that old, for after all, vivid ancestral recollections of Ice Age conditions should surely be followed by at least some accounts from the supposed intervening 8,000 years of those tribes' histories before the beginning of megalithic building.

And because the Olmecs said that they settled in Central America by navigating across the Atlantic when their ancestors could measure the round face of the earth and the arch of the sky in the time of black rain and constant twilight, which therewith reveals a precession-derived mapmaking acumen during the Ice Age, are we therefore to conclude that such occurred during the orthodox 10000 B.C. timeframe when cavemen were supposedly just learning to farm with crude stone tools, and when such Ice Age meteorological conditions were supposedly then soon to end, according to orthodoxy?

Graham Hancock in his book *Underworld* cites what he thinks is a circa 10000 B.C. megalithic community in the foothills of the Hindu Kush Mountains called Merhgarh, which is supposedly one of the earliest evidences of the theorized evolution from a caveman-hunter-gatherer mode of existence, to a centralized farming mode of subsistence, with brick-built communities and grain storage facilities for the bounty of the supposedly then new science of agriculture.[13] The location of Mehrgarh in those foothills of central Pakistan is on what was the western edge of the Indus-Sarasvati civilization, where ruins of brick-buildings are found which look like those at Mehrgarh, therefore, one logically presumes that they are of the same time period which is circa 2000 B.C.

Mainstream scientists base their circa 10000 B.C. date for Mehrgarh on carbon 14 dating results, but carbon 14 dates are notoriously unreliable, particularly those which date organic materials from the time of the Ice Age, because during the Ice Age, all of the volcanoes, thousands of them, spewed prolific volumes of carbon dioxide into the atmosphere. And because that carbon, with which oxygen composes carbon dioxide, is carbon 12, therefore, all of the carbon dioxide from those active Ice Age volcanoes diluted the relative amount of carbon 14 in the atmosphere, so organic materials from the Ice Age show greatly exaggerated carbon 14 dates.

And those thousands of volcanoes which were erupting during the Ice Age blasted prolific volumes of ash into the atmosphere which fell back to earth as black rain, in a time of constant twilight, caused by the dense cloud-cover, combined with all the volcanic ash, during the Ice Age. It was a sooty rain from the water-clouds' admixture with the ash clouds emitted from the volcanoes.

The thought comes to mind, how could precession measurements of the stars with the archaeometer by the ancients have been executed with such dense cloud-cover? Well, the evidence indicates that during the Ice Age, the dense cloud-cover manifested as massive banks of clouds swirling around low pressure areas, and so, there were gaps between cloud-banks as the ice-laden clouds circulated around the zones of low pressure. The ash-clouds from the thousands of volcanoes furthered the murky pale which had enveloped the earth, but one can see that the ancient navigators could pick their spots for precession measurements.

An ancient Turkish legend speaks of the time when the world's first great military leader, Sargon of Agade of Mesopotamia, marched into what was then Hittite territory in Turkey to put down some strife, and the account says that he and his army had to hack through the jungles of eastern Turkey, replete with diverse wild-game and exotic birds.[15] Jungles of eastern Turkey, with prolific and diverse vegetation and wildlife? That region is now quite arid, with no jungles to be found within thousands of miles, and the wildlife there today certainly cannot be described as prolific and diverse.

This same Sargon from circa 2000 B.C. is said to have had a fleet of cargo ships that traded with Melluah,[16] and Melluah is the Mesopotamian name for the Indus-Sarasvati civilization of northwest India and eastern Pakistan, which had port facilities for cargo ships, such as the inland river-port of Lothal, now in a barren desert, and the now submerged cities in the Gulfs of Cambay and Kutch, which no doubt were port cities during the Ice Age when sea level was a few hundred feet lower.

We await further inspection of these vast brick cities on the seafloor there in about 100 feet of water which appear to be like those onshore at Harappa, Mohenjo-Daro, and Lothal, but don't hold your breath for mainstream academia to launch a thorough investigation of these obvious anomalies on that otherwise barren and gently sloping seafloor that are next to ancient and now submerged river beds, for it is quite obvious that they would not like what they would see. The website www.Morien-Institute.org has a fabulous picture of an enhanced sonogram shot of buildings on the seafloor in the Gulf of Cambay, which show irrefutably that we are dealing there with manmade structures, but have we seen these pictures, like those also at www.GrahamHancock.com, on the front page of, say, the New York Times?

Ruins of ancient towns dot the desolate windswept landscapes of the deserts of the Middle East, Egypt, and the northwest India. Are we to believe that those were the sites of thriving societies some 8,000 years after the orthodox date for the end of the Ice Age, at circa 2000 B.C., when the climate was supposedly as it is today? According to mainstream scientists, the lush grasslands and forests caused by the Ice Age climate dried-up about 8,000 years before the date which, virtually all concur, was when these ancient city-states were actually thriving, circa 2000 B.C., so how did they thrive there in what now are seas of sand?

The streams and lakes which once nourished the Middle East are now just a series of ancient lake beds and stream channels beneath the now shifting sands of the desert, which shows that the Ice Age-Middle East was a land of plenty, a land which could support the many ancient city-states, such as Ubar in Oman, and Sippar in Iraq, whose ruins now lie under the shifting sands of the arid and desolate moonscape which is much of the Middle East.

Think about the many tribes of the Bible from around the time of Abraham (circa 2000 B.C.), some of which have been confirmed by modern archaeology, such as the Hittites, the Canaanites (of Canaan, a son of Ham), the Moabites, the Midianites, the Amorites, the Elamites (of Elam, a son of Shem), and the Kaldis (from a son of Arphaxad, who was a son of Shem), all prospered in what is now one of the most desolate desert regions of the world. The hundreds of thousands of citizens of these ancient city-state kingdoms could not have survived with today's current regime of scarce rainfall and resultant vegetation (or lack thereof), which allows settlement today, only because of water wells drilled to considerable depths.

Whereas the Sahara in Africa has but one remnant Ice Age lake (Lake Chad), only because the highlands of Central Africa still supply sufficient rainwater runoff and artesian waters to re-supply the waters of the basin Lake Chad, all of the basins of the Middle East are dried-up, because there are no highlands in that region which hold enough water for streams to re-supply the Ice Age basins there, which were shallow lakes with interconnecting rivers about four thousand years ago. The Great Basin region of Nevada is much the same, with many dried-up Ice Age basin lakes, and the same can be said of the western Gobi Desert, and the Taklamakan Desert which is just north of the Hindu Kush (northeastern Afghanistan and Kashmir) portion of the Himalayas.

The ancient city on the Ice Age lake of the Taklamakan basin was Karakota, which was a thriving trade center during the Ice Age, when trees and grasslands abounded there due to consistent Ice Age precipitation, but now, it is a classic parched and treeless moonscape of windswept sand. Looking at the mountains of wind-blown sand makes it difficult to imagine a once thriving trade-center there, on a vast lake surrounded by rolling hills of grasslands and forests, but such was the scene when Karakota thrived as a way-station on the ancient Silk Road, the trade route which is said to have begun by one of the very earliest Chinese emperors, Emperor Shun.

There are gigantic megalithic stone-circles in these now parched and desolate areas of the ancient world, like those of the ancient Moabites on the top of their hilltop fortress-city at al-Murayghat in desolate central Jordan, and like those:

> *Between the Persian Gulf and the Red Sea, in the district of Kasin (in Arabia), are reported three huge rude Stone Circles, which are described as being "Like Stonehenge" and, like it, composed of gigantic trilithons about fifteen feet high; and several huge Stone Circles in the neighbourhood of Mr. Sinai (in northwest Arabia), and some of them measuring one-hundred feet in diameter. On the old caravan route from the Cilician coast via "Jonah's Pillar" to Persia (or Iran of the ancient sun-worshippers), several megaliths are incidentally reported by travelers. Near Tabriz, to the east of Lake Van (near Ararat), are "several circles" of gigantic stones ascribed to the giants "Caous" (Cassi) of the Kainan (Canaan) dynasty. In Parthia at Deh Ayeh near Darabgerd, is a large circle. On the N.W. frontier of India, on the route from Persia near Peshawar, is a large circle of unhewn megaliths about eleven feet high, and resembling the great Keswick Circle in Cumberland (Britain). And amongst the many megaliths along the Mediterranean coast of Africa, so frequented by the Phoenicians (from Canaan), are several Stone Circles in Tripoli and the Gaet-uli hills with trilithons, like Stonehenge.*[17]

The just referred-to trilithons of the stone-circles in Tunisia are said to be like those at Stonehenge in southern England, and those at Stonehenge are five pairs of huge upright stones that are planted in a U-shaped grouping, with a lintel (crosspiece) over each pair, and around this U-shaped construction are the massive upright megaliths that make-up the notable ring of megaliths which one sees from afar at Stonehenge.

These trilithons look just like the symbol for Pi(and the Greek and Russian letter for the letter p is the pi sign), and as demonstrated with Appendix 1, the ancients were knowledgeable about such geometric truths, and so, it is conceivable that the sign for pi is a picture of these trilithons, whose utilization by the ancient settlers in England helped them to mark precession time, and to mark the solar equinoxes and solstices.

These stone-circles with trilithons were places of worship where they marveled-at and measured the apparent movement of the houses of the zodiac along the horizon through the centuries (in a counter-clockwise direction) because of the slow wobble of the earth's axis, and where they measured the movement of the sun through the houses of the zodiac through a year (in a clockwise direction), because of the annual rotation of the earth around the sun.

The hilltop stone-circle ceremonial complex of the ancient Moabite fortress-city at al-Murayghat in the barren treeless steppes of central Jordan is a testimony that the Ice Age climate must have allowed that city of huge megalithic walls and twenty or so megalithic buildings to flourish in what now looks like a parched moonscape. This was the center of the Moabite civilization, with tens of thousands of civilians, so there is no way that the current climate allowing the present sparse flora and fauna could have supported the nation of Moab.

Because the many other stone-circles in the now parched reaches of the Middle East, North Africa, and the Indus-Sarasvati regions were obviously near or within population centers, due to the stone-circles' religious ceremonial significance to the ancient nations, it is clear that only the rainfall of the Ice Age could have sustained flora and fauna sufficient for the many hundreds of thousands (if not millions) of people who populated, built, farmed, herded, and hunted, on those now desolate (but then lush) desert regions of the earth.

8

CHAPTER

Earth Hexagon Architecture and the Zodiac

The Great Pyramid of the Giza Plateau in Egypt is the monument to the ancients' earth-measuring ability, and this ability was predicated upon their establishment of a hexagon circumscribed by the circle of the earth, with which they measured the distances which the constellations would appear to move along the horizon, because of the slow wobble of the earth's axis, like a gyroscope in space, that would cycle once in 25,920 years.

The hexagon for the ancient mapping system, and thereby, for our modern system, is a six-sided polygon, and therefore, as we have seen the variety of base 6 denominated precession numbers (such as 12, 36, 54, 72, etc.) which are integral to many architectural designs and legends of various ancient people-groups, so we therewith see a widespread knowledge about this astronomical mapping methodology throughout the ancient world that is matched by the widespread coverage of the ancient Ice Age maps, which were drawn with ancient precession-measured geographical data. The hexagon is the linchpin for this mapping and timekeeping system, so we predictably see the hexagon design of architectural motifs in various parts of the world.

The Ice Age Canaanites (and Egyptians) from around 2000 B.C. apparently built the Temple at Baalbeck in the mountains of Lebanon that was composed of incredibly gigantic hewn-megalithic blocks (up to one-thousand tons), some of which remain there today. The style of the massive hewn-megalithic blocks resembles those now submerged off the coast of Lebanon (ancient Yarmuta) and off Egypt at Alexandria, and the sun god of Canaanites was Baal (the namesake of Baalbeck), so the Temple complex was apparently a collaboration between these two ancient Mediterranean cultures in their earliest days during the Ice Age, as they no doubt were cooperating on several levels.

The presence of a hexagonal courtyard within the Baalbeck temple complex[1] is not surprising because the Phoenicians were of Canaan, whose seaports of Sidon, Tyre, and Yarmuta were only a few miles to the southwest of Baalbeck on the Mediterranean coast. From these ports the Phoenicians set sail on their adventures of precession navigating to the distant portions of the globe, equipped with their archaeometers which pinpointed their locations by the position of the stars vis-à-vis those stars' projected future positions along the circular horizon, which when mathematically framed upon the earth hexagon, symbolized with the hexagon court of the Baalbeck temple complex, allowed the ancients to measure the earth, and then worship this knowledge through religious symbolism.

The Canaanite Phoenicians sailed all over the globe in search of tin and copper (and other minerals) to make bronze during the Ice Age. The Phoenicians had far-flung mining operations in Spain, England, Indonesia, Australia,[2] and North America, although the extensive ancient Phoenician copper mines of the Great Lakes were actually developed after the Ice Age icepack had melted off of North America at around 1500 B.C. These Ice Age Phoenician navigators were the Tyranean Sea Fish spoken of in Chapter 3, whose maps were recovered from the Great Library at Alexandria by the Franks, and taken to Constantinople at around 600 A.D., and later were compiled by the Turkish and Portuguese admirals, just before the Renaissance in the 1400's and 1500's A.D.

Remember that those medieval Turkish compilations of the

maps from the Tyranean Sea Fish of Phoenicia (Canaan) show geographical accuracies which would not be matched until the 1800's A.D. with the invention and use of the Harrison's chronometer, the device which "for the first time" allowed navigators to measure east to west distances (longitudes) with great accuracy. It is commonly acknowledged that north-south distance-measurements by the ancients were somewhat accurate because they measured the position of the sun on the horizon through the year relative to visible landmarks.

But east-west distance measurements on maps drawn by the Greeks and Romans were absurdly inaccurate, while the maps of the Tyranean Sea Fish rested anonymously in the Library at Alexandria, apparently unbeknownst to those occupying forces of Greece and Rome, although Ptolemy did "correct" some of the ancient and much more accurate sea king maps. The Tyranean Sea Fish of ancient Phoenicia (Canaan) dominated the high seas for nearly two-thousand years, and this is evident by the many Phoenician rock engravings and settlement-ruins in disparate tin and copper-rich areas of the world,[3] the Greeks and Romans were amateurish navigators in comparison.

Some Roman artifacts have been reported in the Americas, but those may well have been merely trade-barter for the Phoenicians because the Romans never seemed to have any knowledge about the Americas, which is not surprising since the Phoenicians were very jealous of their accurate precession-measured maps, and since they made almost everybody-else believe that if you sailed too far, you'd fall off the edge of the earth, or you would be eaten by hideous sea monsters. They had a real scam on going.

Along with the hexagonal courtyard at the Canaanite Baalbeck, with its inherent base 6 earth-measuring significance, were also the 54 columns,[4] which we have seen is an often-noted precession-derived number of legends and architectures from various ancient cultures, so the ancient knowledge about precession and the methodology for the math which prescribed the precession-derived dimensions for the Great Pyramid of Giza, and thereby, for the accurate mapping and extensive navigation of the globe, are also apparent in the architectural numbers of Baalbeck.

Again in the ancient land of Canaan of circa 2000 B.C., on the Golan Heights at Rujm al-Hiri, was built a megalithic observatory comprised of a series of walls, stone-circles, and stone ellipses which cover about a square block, of which Archaeo News (7 May 2003) reported that:

> *Calculations by Dr. Yoni Mizrachi and colleagues suggested that the openings in the walls allowed the first rays of the sun at the midsummer solstice to pass from the northwestern gate to the centre of the complex. Two stones, 2 metres high by 5 metres wide, allowed the ancients to determine the precession of the equinoxes. Dr Mizrachi has conjectured that the site as a whole relates to star positions at the time of its construction. Similarity with the form of Stonehenge and other sites in England and France caused a wave of speculation when Rujm al-Hiri was first surveyed in 1967-68.*[5]

Notice that Dr. Mizrachi said that precession determinations were executed with this megalithic set-up at Rujm al-Hiri that is like the Stonehenge set-up, and like other megalithic stone-circle set-ups like those also in France at Carnac for instance. These stone-circles of astronomical measuring purposes were common in the ancient world, and such a megalithic facility near the precession numbered temple at Baalbeck, both of which are in the ancient land of the Canaanites, indicates precession measuring with the hexagon as the measuring matrix upon which the measurements were hung, so to speak, by the precession-mapping Phoenicians (Canaanites) and their surveying, building, and navigating cohorts, the Egyptians.

Dr. Mizrachi also said that the megalithic set-up of the Canaanites relates to the star-precession positions at the time of construction around 2000 B.C. This is because the megaliths of those stone-circles were placed to mark stars' positions on the horizon as those stars appeared on the horizon circa 2000 B.C. Mizrachi obviously noticed that some important stars of particular constellations to the Canaanites (the article doesn't say which stars) have moved along the horizon because of precession for about four-thousand years to their present position from the position in which they appeared to the Canaanites at around 2000 B.C, when they were building that precession-measuring megalithic facility.

Similarly, the four diagonal "star shafts" within the Great Pyramid are aligned to the circa 2200 B.C. positions of the dragon star (Alpha Draconis) and the little bear star (Ursa Minor) in the north. And in the south, the Dog Star of Isis (Sirius) and a star of the belt of Orion (Zeta Orionis) are memorialized with the alignments of the star shafts toward those stars as they appeared in the sky some four-thousand years ago.[6] So here we have yet another evidence that the earliest megalithic structures were built around 2000 B.C., but not built one or two (or five) millennia before that time, when some like Graham Hancock are saying that megalithic building really began.

As discussed previously, this is an attempt by some mainstream ancient chronologists to move back the dates for megalithic building to accommodate the reality that when the Ice Age ended and sea level rose, some of these megaliths were submerged, so the orthodox-timeline folks are trying to move up the date for the end of the Ice Age from about 10000 B.C, in order to overlap this necessitated and torturous extension-back for the date of the beginning of the megalithic building projects by the ancients.

The presence of the seafloor megaliths has forced orthodox academicians to begin to attempt to push back the date by 4,000 years for the start of megalithic building (from about 3000 B.C., back to circa 7000 B.C.), and the reality of the submerged megaliths has therewith also necessitated that the orthodox types try to move-up the date for the end of the Ice Age by about 4,000 years (from 10000 B.C., up to circa 6000 B.C.), in order to manipulatively allow a thousand years for the now-submerged megaliths to have been built between 7000 B.C. and 6000 B.C., and subsequently, to have been engulfed by the risen sea level at the end of the Ice Age, supposedly at around 6000 B.C. Talk about massaging the data.

Before this massaging of the data was necessary to synchronize mainstream notions about the relative chronologies of the time of the Ice Age's end vis-à-vis the time of the beginning of ancient megalithic building, the supposed crude nomadic hunter-gatherers of circa 7000 B.C., who are thought to have been barely capable of rubbing two sticks together, and who were purportedly just figuring out that seeds could be stuck into the ground to be expected to grow-up into plants for food, these were the ancient people who we are now expected to believe to have been capable of such impressive megalithic building projects.

And in the minds of the orthodox archaeologists, these quasi-cavemen had yet to figure-out how to smelt copper and tin to make bronze. They were a supposedly a crude lot, using merely sticks and rocks as tools, but not nearly capable of precisely hewing and transporting megalithic blocks up to one-thousand tons into their places as components of ancient astronomically-related temples, pyramids, and stone-circles. But because of the submerged megaliths, mainstream academic chicanery must be called upon to avoid the unthinkable (to them) notion that the Ice Age actually ended circa 1500 B.C., as so much evidence clearly indicates.

The ancient Egyptian god of the dead, one of the children of the sun, was Osiris, who was represented by the constellation Orion (the Hunter), to which was aligned one of the southwardly-aimed shafts of the Great Pyramid, which was built about 4,000 years ago, when the ancients were transitioning from the age of Taurus into the age of Aries because of the slow precession-caused apparent movement of the constellations' positions at dawn on the horizon, such that the spring equinox sun resides in a new "house" every 2,160 years as the 25,920 years per slow wobble of the earth's axis progresses through its cycle of twelve constellations.

This god Osiris was said to have been killed by 72 conspirators, and then his queen Isis put his remains in a floating chest, and off he went down the Nile to end-up at Baalbeck,[7] where was the Canaanite temple dedicated to Baal, the sun god, with its hexagonal courtyard of base 6 mathematical significance. Now let's multiply 6 times 72 to get 4,320, and so discover the number of years that it takes for constellations to appear to move along one side of the earth hexagon because of the slow wobble of the earth's axis. Refer again to Appendix 1, and see that the Great Pyramid is a 1/43,200th scale model of a pyramid which would fit inside a hemisphere of the earth.

The ancient megalithic stone-circle complex on the Golan Heights which Dr. Mizrachi notes to have been a facility for precession measuring was in the ancient land of the Canaanites, the same ancient nation which built the nearby astronomically significant temple of Baalbeck with its 6-sided courtyard to which the Egyptian god of the dead Osiris floated in a chest, after he had been killed by 72 conspirators.

The 12 tribes of the Hebrews conquered most of Canaan around 1400 B.C. after the Hebrews had sojourned out of Egypt at the end of the Ice Age circa 1500 B.C., but they did not touch the Phoenician port cities of Tyre and Sidon, nor the temple of Baalbeck to the north, all three of which are in current-day Lebanon (though some of the ancient port facilities such as of Yarmuta and old Sidon are now submerged just offshore there).

The ancient now-submerged Phoenician port city of Yarmuta, found just offshore of Lebanon, north of Tyre and Sidon, is mentioned in ancient Egyptian texts up until around 1400 B.C., which is a rough date, as we are dealing here with the consequences of Manetho's ancient Egyptian king's list which shows an inaccurate chronology because he counted non-kings as kings, and because he listed contemporaneously ruling city-state "kings" as being sequential rulers over all of Egypt, so a date for the submergence of Yarmuta at the end of the Ice Age near 1500 B.C. certainly fits the fact that port city is now on the seafloor.

Not as much isostatic rebound occurred in the Mediterranean (closer to the Ice Age icepack) at the end of the Ice Age, so sea level did not rise as much there as in the more middle latitudes, and the slope of the seafloor from shore is usually quite steep in the Mediterranean, so less area of land was submerged when the sea level rose, but many submerged ruins in that region such as of Malta, Egypt, and Lebanon, bear silent testimony to the sea level's encroachment upon these civilizations after they had evidently been developed at around 2000 B.C., and not at around 10000 B.C., as orthodox dogma would dictate.

There were six gigantic columns within the sun temple at Baalbeck,[8] which further attests to their surveying and mapping savvy, based upon the notion of the earth hexagon to measure the earth, and thereby, to accurately map and navigate much of the world during the Ice Age. These Phoenician-Canaanites were sailing to and settling much of ice-free portions along the coasts of Europe and North America during the Ice Age, as well as, sailing to the east (perhaps from ports in Arabia) to also settle for mining profit in the islands of southern Asia and Australia.

The Olmecs of African Manding (Banbara)[9] language affinity, with their base six mapping knowledge, were sailing from North Africa to the Central America, and the Egyptians, with their mapping knowledge and seaworthy and sea-worn ships up to one-hundred-forty feet long, were apparently plying the high seas, and as we shall soon see, the people of the ancient cultures of India and the Jomon of eastern Asia were sailing to the east and settling across the Pacific to South America, where some founded the great Andes civilization, commonly referred to as the ancient pre-Inca empire.

The temple of Osiris at Abydos on the Nile in central Egypt, and the Valley Temple at Giza, with their Ice Age rainfall-caused erosion features, had support pillars for the temple roof which are grouped in sixes around the sides of these structures, and so we see more of this ancient intellectual preoccupation with the number six of the earth hexagon, and with the precise astronomically-derived surveying capability which is demonstrated with the dimensions of the Giza Pyramid, and there-from, with the maps of the ancient sea kings.

Like the hexagonal courtyard of the Canaanite temple complex at Baalbeck, but to the east by some one thousand miles, beyond Mesopotamia (Babylon), is the ancient hexagonal dome of Danial-e-Nabi[10] from the ancient Elamite civilization of southern Iran at Susa, that is about five-hundred miles east of Babylon in a parched and inhospitable environment which must have been much wetter when that great ancient Elamite culture was flourishing there at around 2000 B.C. Also of that ancient Elamite region, which is about half-way between Mesopotamia and the Indus region, is the temple of Apadana with its precession-derived number 72 columns.[11]

According to Old Testament history, Elam was a brother of Arphaxad, and I have read that Arphaxad was the father of Kaldi,[12] who became the namesake of the ancient nation of famously proficient astronomers, called Chaldea, also known as Babylonia, so the hexagonal theme of the domed shrine at Danial-e-Nabi of the Elamites is consistent with the base six knowledge within this ancient family lineage, and even orthodox archaeologists credit the Babylonians as being the originators of base six mathematics and astronomical science, so the link is obvious.

The mark of the ancient Hindu god Vishnu is the six-sided hexagon, and the six-sided hexagram of the sacred relic which is the Satkona Yantra of the ancient Tamils of southern India reflects the connections between a great Hindu god, the hexagon, and the most sacred of ancient relics, which is said to hold great power, and which is rarely allowed to be viewed by the public. The Saktona Yantra hexagram is cut into a black stone, with flames cut-in around the circumference of this hexagram.

The ancient Tamil god of this hexagram is Arumukam (which means having six faces), who was a god of fire, and who apparently was also the god of the cycles of time because the Hindu yuga time-periods are multiples of the base 6 number 432,000 which was obviously derived from precession measurements by the ancients with the archaeometer. And the number 432 also relates to the astronomically-derived dimensions of the Great Pyramid, and to the warriors of Valhalla, and also, as the Babylonian historian Berosus of circa 300 B.C. (who compiled the Babylonian king's list) wrote that the pre-Flood kings' reigns totaled 432,000 years, it is plain that precession measuring under-girded many of the traditions of the ancient world.

The Babylonians believed that the creation of the heavens and the earth occurred 432,000 years of kings' reigns before the Great Flood, when "wind blew, torrent and tempest and flood overwhelmed the world, tempest and flood raged together like warring hosts," as described in the Epic of Gilgamesh, which is thought to have been written circa 2000 B.C. And according to the ancient Babylonians, there were ten pre-Flood kings who ruled through those 432,000 years since the time of the creation of the heavens and the earth to the time of the Deluge.

It should be apparent that the odds of that number being an accurate historical number of years from the creation to the Flood are astronomically long compared to the odds that the selection of the number 432 was actually based upon archaeometer measurements of the rate of the precession of the earth's axis, as manifested by the measurable movement along the horizon of the constellations, and as noted, 72 years/degree of precession times 6 sides of the earth hexagon equals 432, and remember that is the operative number for the miniaturization of the dimensions of the earth that was achieved with the astronomically-derived dimensions of the Great Pyramid of Giza.

Think about it, the ancient 432,000 year-denominated yugas of time of the Hindus, and the Babylonian 432,000 years of pre-Flood kings' reigns, could not have literally been counted by humans, because who would say that supposedly evolving monkey-men of 432,000 years ago were then counting periods of time between global catastrophes (or from the creation)? According to mainstream archaeologists, humans weren't counting much over ten fingers and ten toes at the end of the Ice Age, which they say ended at around 10000 B.C., so you can see that the disconnect between the archaeological record and this, actually precession-based, number of 432,000 years of supposed humanly-counted time is irreconcilable.

The ancient Babylonians (specifically the Chaldeans, from Kaldi, a son of Arphaxad) were notorious religio-astronomers, and everyone agrees that they founded and propagated the religion of astrology which is based upon the 12 constellations' apparent slow movement along the horizon as the sun moves into a new "house" every 2,160 years because of the slow wobble of the earth's axis. And this earth's axis is allegorized as the World Tree in many ancient cultures, which shakes convulsively when the sun enters a new house. This is why we have the legendary catastrophes at base 6 denominated periods of years in Hinduism, and why the Babylonians picked a base 6 number multiple of years between the creation and the Deluge.

The Temple of Dendera with 6 columns in front has also a mural inside of the 12 Egyptian constellations of the zodiac, so you see there symbolized are the 6 sides of the earth hexagon, as well as the 6 columns times 2 which results in the number 12 of subdivisions of the earth hexagon which are of 2,160 year lengths which are half of the 4,320 years that it takes for the constellations to move along one side of the earth hexagon. And of course, that number 4,320 is the basis for the miniaturization-ratio prescribed for the dimensions of the Great Pyramid of Giza.

About six thousand miles to the east of Egypt are the islands of Japan which are the remnants of the ancient land of the Jomon civilization that was partially submerged when the sea level rose at the end of the Ice Age to cover what was then a large peninsula which connected to mainland China at the southwestern portion of Japan. Remember too that the Ice Age maps which were compiled by the great Chinese cartographers show the nearby Yellow Sea being then much smaller when the sea level was lower during the Ice Age.

We have seen that the Jomon were advanced megalithic builders during the Ice Age, as evidenced with the rock-hewn tiered-plazas, stone-circles, and megalithic walls which are now on the seafloor due to the sea level rise at the end of the Ice Age, so it is problematic for mainstream scientists to rationalize their timeline for the Jomon civilization as supposedly lasting from around 15000 B.C. to 2000 B.C. because the pottery, architecture, and modes of construction did not change for the supposed 13,000 years of Jomon development.

Graham Hancock himself admits that the advanced building styles exhibited at the ancient north-of-Tokyo Jomon ruin site of Sannai-Muryama are of circa 2000 B.C. vintage, with wide streets, spacious public buildings, and sanitation systems (sounds like the ancient Indus cities, doesn't it?), so the fact that there is no orthodox-predicted evidence of 13,000 years of cultural and architectural evolution to the advanced tool-hewn megalithic structures of Jomon civilization, both on land, as at Sannai-Muryama, and now submerged, as off the Japanese islands of Yonaguni, Kerama, and Chatan, on the southwestern end of the Ice Age Japanese peninsula, these show that the Jomon people appeared and developed their civilization suddenly at around 2000 B.C. during the Ice Age.

And then some of those megalithic structures were engulfed when the sea level rose to submerge the legendary kingdom of the ancient Japanese sea god, down to which the hero Fire-Fade of the ancient Japanese book the Nihongi sank in a basket to retrieve his fishing hook:

> *Forthwith he found himself at a pleasant strand, where he abandoned the basket, and, proceeding on his way, suddenly arrived at the Palace of the Sea God. This palace was provided with battlements and turrets, and stately towers.*

Hancock duly notes that this description remarkably matches some of the submerged megalithic structures which are found off Kerama and Chatan near Taiwan, and also, please know that with those building structures are stone-circles which look like the many ones still onshore that are commonly dated to circa 2000 B.C., not to circa 10000 B.C., as orthodox scientists would surmise because the Jomon supposedly had been around since 15000 B.C.

Excavations south of Tokyo at Chichamori Iseki have exposed the remains of two large "wood-henges" which are considered to be vintage Jomon astronomical-measuring circle-work of circa 2000 B.C., whose uprights consisted of 12 huge chestnut trees arranged in a circle. Here we have again that number 12 of zodiac constellations now represented in this design of an ancient Jomon astronomical measuring site.

The 6 sided hexagon of the circle of the earth is the basis of the 12 constellations of the zodiac because each "housing" of the sun provided by the 12 respective constellations would last 2,160 years, which is one-half of the 4,320 years that it takes for the constellations to appear to move along one side of the earth hexagon because of precession, therefore, as 6 sides of the hexagon times 2 equals 12 constellations, and as 2,160 years per "housing" times 2 equals the time 4,320 years along one side of the hexagon, we see that the zodiac concept derives directly from the base 6 earth mapping scheme, which is encapsulated with the astronomically-derived dimensions of the Great Pyramid of Giza. (Refer to Appendix 1 for a refresher.)

The symbol for the earth in Taoism (Tao means the path) is the hexagon, and hexagon-shaped ancient tombs have been found in Japan, so it seems that the east Asians were well versed in the base six methodology for the math used to astronomically derive earth distances, and so they memorialized in their ceremonial symbolism this unique polygon with which one can measure the earth. This is a truly marvelous geometric shape which is also the linchpin shape for computer science and organic chemistry.

All of nature seems formed upon hexagonal matrices of fantastic design, and the precession of the constellations occurs in an orderly and predictable way, which can be applied for earth distances through knowledge about the nature of the earth hexagon as it relates to the radius-length of the earth, and therefore, as it relates to the circumference-length of the earth. The natural world is obviously of a grand design which humans have successfully quantified through an awareness of the hexagonal matrices of the systems which comprise the creation.

And the pervasiveness in the ancient world of base six numbering, the hexagonal symbolism, and the base six number twelve constellations of the zodiac that permeated many of the ancient cultures, bear stark witness to the far-ranging ancient knowledge of the precession measuring, which allowed them to accurately map and navigate much of the globe during the Ice Age.

9

CHAPTER

Sea Kings Navigated the Pacific

On the seafloor near the island of Yonaguni of the Ryuku Islands (named after the Ice Age King Riujin) of southwestern Japan are some of the submerged Jomon megaliths which are of form and function characteristic of the 2000 B.C. vintage construction techniques of the Jomon, and among those submerged since 1500 B.C. ruins is a stone-circle, and in the middle of that particular megalithic circle is a hexagonal megalithic pillar,[1] which in combination obviously reveal the base six precession-measuring acumen of these Ice Age settlers on what was then not a series of islands, but was a continuous strip of land, when sea level was a few hundred feet lower, during the Ice Age.

The layout of the now-submerged hexagonal pillar and stone-circle jibes with the base 6 mapping scheme of the ancients, and jibes with the 12 constellations of the east Asian zodiac (which were all seen as animals by the ancient east Asians), because as we have seen, the number 12 of constellations, recognized by all the ancient earth-measuring cultures, is merely 2 times the 6 sides of the earth hexagon, for the total of 12 constellations which seem to move slowly along the horizon, because of the slow wobble of the earth's axis, like a gyroscope in space, which would complete one wobble in 25,920 years.

And this number twelve of zodiac constellations is mirrored with the so-called Twelve Winds Maps which are some of the Turkish medieval maps compiled from the ancient source maps from the ancient Phoenicians, the Tyranean Sea Fish, via the ancient Library of Alexandria, from where the maps were spirited away to Constantinople (Istanbul) about the year 600 A.D. when the library founded by Alexander the Great at Alexandria was destroyed.

These maps are like the Piri Reis Map of 1513 A.D., and like the other amazingly accurate medieval maps discussed in Chapter 3, but rather than having "eight winds" of same-length spokes radiating from a reference point on a map, these Twelve Winds Maps show twelve spokes radiating from a given reference point, and so plainly parrot the zodiac precession-measuring inherent to the ancient studies of astronomy and astrology which are generally credited to have originated and been propagated by the Chaldeans of embryonic Babylon, who obviously had shared this knowledge with the Canaanites and the Egyptians. The eight winds medieval maps were apparently drawn from ancient maps, but the spokes were "modernized" to the cardinal direction layout, rather than to the original hexagon mapping system, as the knowledge of the ancient precession mapping technique was all but lost.

The number of the eight winds map results from multiplying the four cardinal directions by two, whereas, the Twelve Winds Maps result from multiplying the six sides of the earth hexagon by two, and so, the Twelve Winds Maps reflect the pure essence of the precession-derived method for the demonstrably accurate charting of the earth by the ancient sea kings. The twelve winds track the twelve constellations, so to speak, and thereby, we see that mapping, time-reckoning, and the precession of the constellations of the zodiac, are interlinked by their unique shared essence.

In his wonderful chronicle about what then (before this book, *Ice Age Civilizations*) was a great mystery surrounding the fabulously accurate *Maps of the Ancient Sea Kings*, author Charles H. Hapgood ponders over the apparent commonality of this then mysterious methodology which was utilized by the great ancient seafaring cultures of the world. I have taken the liberty to quote him here at some length, to show that this great historian of cartography saw that there was a method to the ancient mapping phenomenon, but he just couldn't put his finger on it:

> *Now, from the standpoint of the history of science, the twelve-wind system is of very special importance. This system involved, as we have previously pointed out, the division of the circle into twelve arcs of 30 degrees each, or six arcs of 60 degrees. It involved the division of the circle into 360 degrees. This fact relates the system, in most interesting fashion, to Babylonian science. The Babylonians had a numbering system based on sixty, and on decimals. They are supposed to have invented the 360-degree circle, and the divisions of time we still use today.*
>
> *The Babylonians also had a zodiac, and this was divided into twelve signs of 30 degrees each. The constellations of the zodiac did not precisely coincide with the twelve signs, as was natural enough, since the latter were mathematical divisions.*
>
> *Now the stars were used in ancient times, in navigation, as E. G. R. Taylor points out, and so the zodiac and the other constellations of the northern and southern hemisphere were a sort of map written in the sky. The relationships of the Babylonians and Phoenicians in ancient times were very close, and we can easily imagine that the Phoenicians might have applied these basic elements of Babylonian science to mapmaking. The result of any such effort would have been the twelve-wind system.*
>
> *There are curious connections and comparisons that can be made between the ancient sciences of Greece, Egypt, Babylonia, and China, not to neglect either India*

or Central America. I have assembled some passages referring to these connections, showing particularly that both the Babylonians and the Chinese had numbering systems that could fit in very well with decimals of the twelve-wind system.[2]

Professor Hapgood passed-away a few years ago, but had he not, I would have certainly forwarded to him a copy of this book, as his quandary is herewith solved because I have explained how the ancients measured precession with the archaeometer, and then applied those measurements to the hexagon of the circle of the earth, and thereby, were able to precisely chart distances and directions, as evidenced with the marvelously accurate ancient maps, about which Hapgood pondered.

The medieval Cantino Map of 1502 A.D., which was also based on ancient source maps, shows that the now shallow seafloor of the Sunda Shelf around Sumatra, Java, Borneo, and Malaysia was part of a huge peninsula that extended south from Asia[3] during the Ice Age when the sea level was about 300 feet lower. These large islands today were the high ground on the Ice Age Sunda Shelf peninsula, and now are the remnants of the sea level rise which engulfed about 25 million square miles of land at the close of the Ice Age around 1500 B.C.

Medieval Portuguese navigators, who had also accessed the ancient source maps saved at Constantinople, sailed into south Asian seas using the Cantino Map, but encountered a series of big islands,[4] not the huge peninsula which was shown on the compilation of ancient maps. This map covers India, the Indian Ocean to its east, and the exposed Sunda Shelf even farther to the east. India is depicted much more accurately on this map than could medieval cartographical expertise muster, so the Sunda Shelf mapping would be presumed to be so accurate, which it is, but accurate for the Ice Age era when so much of the seafloor of the Sunda Shelf was exposed land, whereas at that time, a much smaller percentage of India had yet to submerge, much of it around northwestern and southern India as we have seen.

It is evident that the precession navigators were sailing around the Sunda Shelf peninsula during the Ice Age, and that ancient land, known as Golden Chersonese, or Sundaland, or the lost continent of Mu (in some New Age circles), a land which the natives say was mostly engulfed by the sea long ago, is now on the shallow seafloor of the Sunda Shelf. This region should be a prime hunting ground for submerged megaliths because the megalithic pyramids on the remnant islands corroborate an ancient civilization there, so we should expect similar structures on the shallow seafloor there, as are found from the Indus-Sarasvati, Tamil/Dravidian, Egyptian, Canaanite, and Jomon civilizations.

The northeast portion of the Sunda Shelf provides shallow seafloor off the coast of Vietnam and off the southeast coast of China which includes the waters off Taiwan and the nearby Japanese islands, where are found the submerged Jomon megalithic structures of Kerama, Yonaguni, and Chatan, all of which are near Okinawa at the southwestern end of the Japanese archipelago, the area called the Ryukyu Islands. And the ancient megalithic architectures, both on land and seafloor,[5] greatly resemble the architectures of ancient structures found on the remnant islands (such as Borneo, Java, and Sumatra) of the mostly now submerged Sundaland, or Golden Chersonese, the "lost continent of Mu."

The Jomon civilization of Sundaland is considered to be a subset of the so-called Lapita culture, which orthodox archaeologists admit must have been a people of incredible navigators, as they spread their megalithic building-style which greatly resembles the sweeping rock-hewn tiered ceremonial plazas, platforms, and walls of finely-hewed and fitted-rock walls throughout the Pacific,[6] and even to South America, where they built the great megalithic tiered-plazas, platforms, massive fitted polygonal-rock walls, and astronomically-aligned ceremonial stones such as those of Machu Pichu.

This ancient seafaring Lapita culture also produced excellent pottery with tell-tale decorative designs which further evidence the wide diffusion of the Lapita people throughout the Pacific. The word Jomon refers to the braided imprints around the rim of their pottery, and this type of design is common at ancient sites throughout the Pacific, some having been found in the Andes[7] and the Baja peninsula.[8]

We saw in Chapter 1 that the ancients cut boulders and rock formations with a bronze saw whose teeth were composed of replaceable mineral crystals which were known to be harder than the rock to be cut, and then, soaked wooden wedges were inserted along the saw-cut to expand and separate the rock. This simple rock-cutting technique could very well have been virtually universal during the Ice Age, as wood and bronze were all that was needed, and so, the cutting of the blocks of rock to create the ceremonial megalithic tiered-plazas, and ramps, and finely hewn and tightly-fitted megalithic walls can be explained. In addition:

> *A profound connection between Taiwan, the Ryukus, and China is evidenced in combination of chipped and partially polished rectangular hoes, stepped adzes, and shouldered axes... these could have been used to modify stone surfaces and territory for commerce or build terrace agriculture.*[9]

The problem of lifting the massive rock-hewn blocks of sometimes hundreds of tons remains a mystery, but one can envision a sort of counter-balance machine, like a teeter-totter, where weight could be added to the counter-side until the megalithic block lifted. Several such machines applied to a super-megalithic block could account for such engineering marvels as those of Baalbeck of the Canaanites, the megaliths of Malta, the temples and walls of Egypt, and of the Jomon, and the massive walls and buildings of monstrous megalithic blocks at Tiahuanaco in the Andes of Bolivia near Lake Titicaca:

> *Terrace cultures were at one time also prominent in South America. NASA satellite photographs of Tiahuanaco, Bolivia in the late 1980's revealed an extensive, yet forgotten, array of stone patterns and*

platforms which were recently determined to have been built by early cultures to manage a sophisticated irrigation system at high altitudes These platforms are adjacent to ancient monuments and structures that served as ceremonial centers, exhibiting sun and stellar alignments, as well as containing water conduits for ceremonial rituals. And what about the Mayan culture with their, platforms, sun worship rituals and astronomically aligned structures?

One can argue that in the Chinese architectural tradition of temple platforms, vertical discrimination of space was three-fold, including ground level neutral planes elevated or positive planes represented by platforms, and pits or negative planes represented by sunken courts. Most sunken courts had aligned flights of stairs on opposite sides, one for descent and the other for ascent, designed for ritual procession into and out of negative space. Yonaguni tombs in the coastal regions imitate the same step functions found on the submerged platforms, viz., two or three steps, usually of different heights, connecting each platform horizon in elevated or sunken space on one side with great systemization of space. A similar three-tiered symbolic structure can also be found throughout South America."[10]

The preceding two paragraphs are quotes from a paper which was co-authored by Dr. Robert Schoch of Boston University who, as we have seen, correctly propones that the anomalously great amount of rain erosion on the limestone manmade structures of Egypt indicates that those structures existed during the Ice Age, but who wrongly goes along with orthodox scientists that the Ice Age ended around 10000 B.C., or somewhat after that date.

Schoch and Graham Hancock, among others, are trying to move up the date for the end of the Ice Age, while they try to move back the date for the beginning of the advanced megalithic building, to reconcile the rain-eroded buildings on land, and now-submerged megalithic buildings, with the time of the end of the Ice Age, through a torturous manipulation of the orthodox timeline. As I said before, watch for more of their necessitated orthodox timeline-fudging to reconcile this anomalous (to them) archaeological evidence.

They aren't having much luck moving back the date for the megalithic building, and the following quote from Hancock's own book *Fingerprints of the Gods* expresses the general consensus from orthodox scientists regarding the timing of the end of the Ice Age, so those manipulators of the orthodox timeline are faced with a gaping eight-thousand year plus stretch of time, between what orthodox scientists say was the time of the beginning of the megalithic building, back to when they say was the time of the end of the Ice Age:

> *The rapidity of the de-glaciation (at the end of the Ice Age) suggests that some extraordinary factor was affecting the climate. The dates suggest that this factor first made itself felt about 16,500 years ago, that it had destroyed most, perhaps three-quarters of the glaciers by 2000 years later, and that (the vast bulk of these dramatic developments took place) in a millennium or less.*[11]

Here we have Hancock's own reference which is representative of the mainstream consensus that the melting of the Ice Age icepack was all but over by 12000 B.C., and commensurately, that sea level had pretty-much stopped rising by then, purportedly at least eight thousand years before the supposed time of the building of the now "anomalously" submerged megaliths which are found on the shallow seafloors of the world, near the ruins of similar structures onshore. Hancock published *Fingerprints of the Gods* in 1995, and by the time of his writing of *Underworld* in 2002, he had begun to try to close the gap by fudging the consensus opinions about the date for the end of the Ice Age, and for the supposed time that megalithic building was commenced by the ancients.

Remember that submerged megalithic constructions have been found at hundred foot depths on the seafloor, and there is no reason to think that others are not submerged at even greater depths on those relatively shallow continental shelves, which Milne and others have shown to have been 25 million square miles of dry land during the Ice Age, so all of that coastal dry land which was exposed by the lower sea level during the Ice Age was prime real estate for the ancients to develop.

We have seen that the ancient legends speak of the surprisingly rapid sea level rise within a matter of a few decades that covered the kingdoms of the "Rama Empire" of the Indus-Sarasvati civilization, Kumari Kandam of the Tamil/Dravidian civilization, Gaulometin which was the kingdom now submerged between Malta and Sicily,[12] and Sundaland/Lost Continent of Mu of the so-called Lapita people, of whom were the Jomon of Japan, so it is strange that Hancock does not attempt to rebut that the Ice Age, according to those legends, which he himself has cited in his books, ended within a matter of mere decades, and not slowly over about 8,000 years, from the orthodox date for the beginning of the supposed slow meltdown at about 14000 B.C., all the way to Hancock's uncomfortable yet necessitated date of 6000 B.C., (a date which must be torturously fudged-forward, that far, to overlap with his hoped-for back-dating for the time when megalithic building began to about 7000 B.C.)

Illogical is his unstated but unavoidable inference that most of the roughly three-hundred foot sea level rise from the melting of the Ice Age icepacks occurred at around 6000 B.C., to cover those now submerged megaliths which he hopes can be back-dated to that same timeframe. We have seen that the lion's share of the melting, according to orthodox science, occurred probably within a millennium at around 12000 B.C., so his is a timeline-stretch of flagrantly untenable proportions.

Some of orthodox science will argue that the Ice Age icepack melted in three stages over about 6,000 years, starting at around

14000 B.C., then ending at about 8000 B.C., but the evidence belies this contention, some of this evidence being the ancient legends that the sea level rose within a matter of mere decades. And the contemporaneously built megalithic structures, which are of form and function of circa 2000 B.C, are found still on land, and the lower lying ones were submerged, so those submerged ones could not have been engulfed through 8,000 years, beginning at around 14000 B.C., with the lion's share of the melting having, conveniently for Hancock, occurred within about a thousand years, from 7000 B.C. to 6000 B.C.

In other words, Hancock, Schoch, and others, are trying to sell that the Ice Age icepacks melted over about eight-thousand years (perhaps in three progressive stages), until around 6000 B.C., and that therewith, oddly, almost all of that melting, which caused almost all of the sea level rise of two to three-hundred feet, just happened to have conveniently occurred at the very end of that long period of time, shortly after the now-submerged megaliths were built at the torturously back-dated circa 7000 B.C.

It is ironic that even in 2002 with his book *Underworld*, Hancock cites some interesting information from Dr. John Shaw of the University of Alberta about the rapid meltdown of the Ice Age icepack[13] that belies Hancock's very own thesis that the sea level rose over about eight-thousand years. Hancock says about the massive volumes of water which were produced when the Ice Age icepacks melted:

> *I think it is worth re-emphasizing Shaw's figures and their implications. He is talking about turbulent, energetic floods 20 meters deep, flowing in vortices at high speed and pressure, under the main ice-sheets, across fronts up to 160 kilometers wide. Only floods on such a scale and of such violence could have sculpted the drumlin-fields and hummocky terrain and tortured pitted scablands of Canada and the United States and carved out other remarkable features such the extremely large through valleys—including those containing the Finger Lakes—*

that lie to the south of drumlin-fields in northern New York State. Volumes of water required to sustain such floods, observes Shaw, would have been of the order of one million cubic kilometers equivalent to a rise of the several meters in sea-level over a matter of weeks.[14]

Notice that he said several meters of sea level rise in a matter of weeks. Well now, then that was hundreds of feet of sea level rise in a matter of decades, and that's exactly what I'm talking about, and what I am surprised that Hancock included as evidence that his Ice Age supposedly melted over an eight thousand year period of time. Of course, however, he does seem to claim that almost all of the melting of eight-thousand years strangely occurred at the very end, at around 6000 B.C., which is, conveniently for him, about one thousand years after his torturous back-dating for the commencement of megalithic building to around 7000 B.C.

Imagine the surging torrents of water described by Shaw which came from the melting Ice Age icepacks. Picture the thundering rivers of melt-water surging through and gouging terrain from that rapid melting to supply such volumes of melt-water to pour into the oceans that sea level rose several hundred feet within a matter of decades, as corroborated with the ancient legends previously noted. And many ancient human skeletons are found jumbled with the bones of Ice Age animals in caves where they were flooded-out, obviously, after having sought refuge from the torrents of melt-water which, according to Shaw, were up to fifty feet deep, and which fanned-out near the rising-ocean shoreline to virtually cover the then submerging Ice Age coastal areas with a blanket of melt-water and sediment.

Torrents of melt-water fifty feet deep, flooding-out caves and severely scouring vast swaths of continental landmasses? This hardly sounds like the result of a rate of melting which one would expect from the proposed gradual meltdown, with fits and starts through eight thousand years, where one would expect little-more runoff than that which occurs today in the springtime in the more extreme-latitude continental landmasses which retain snow and ice in the wintertime.

The ancient so-called Lapita culture navigated and settled all over the South Pacific during the Ice Age, usually settling on islands with mineral deposits and pearl/oyster banks just offshore. The ceremonial megalithic tiered-plazas of hewed megalithic blocks[15] are inevitably found where are found ancient mines and known pearl fisheries, as are found on the islands of Tahiti, the Cook Islands, and the Hawaiian islands.[16]

So how do orthodox archaeologists explain the mining by these ancient islanders, and their smelting of tools (which are evidenced with slag-pits), and their advanced megalithic building, and their proficient navigation with their resultant widely dispersed megalithic settlements of islands separated by thousands of miles of imposing seas?

They by and large do not explain such, because there is no rational explanation to answer how it could be that those ancient seafaring settlers of the islands of the Pacific were simple so-called stone-age people, with crude canoes and the navigation tools of a child, who were mindlessly hopeful that puttering off over the horizon of the vast Pacific in their stone-age canoes, with merely the rising sun to tell them which way to go, would be a clever and wise thing to do. With that scenario, it sounds more like a suicide voyage to me.

But as we have seen that some ancient Phoenician mining sites, with megalithic structures of those great precession navigators from around 2000 B.C., are also scattered about the south Pacific, is it therefore too much to see that the ancient seafaring Lapita people, with cultural ties to the precession-conscious and megalithic-building Jomon of east Asia, would also be capable of such navigational skills as had the Phoenicians? Incidentally, it is oxymoronic to say that so-called stone-age people mined and smelted ore to mold metal tools, because since they had done so, they were by definition not stone-age people.

They in fact were highly sophisticated miner/smelters and megalithic builders who therefore had all of the technological savvy of the Phoenicians, and who settled in far-flung lands as did the Phoenicians, and yet, we are expected to believe that the Lapita people puttered along in crude rafts or canoes with a few stone axes and their finger in the wind, ever mindful that the sun rises in the east, but mindful of not much more?

And these Lapita people evidently were the builders of the vast megalithic tiered-platforms and terraced pyramids with astronomically-measured alignments and huge precisely-fitted polygonal megalithic blocks which look like those spread throughout the Pacific islands that were also constructed in the Andes, evidently during the Ice Age, because some of the flooded-out people and Ice Age animals in flood deposits from the end of the Ice Age melt-water are found at Tiahuanaco near Lake Titicaca in Bolivia where there is evidence that the end of the Ice Age flood of melt-water from the mountains surged down the valley and flooded out the civilization at Tiahuanaco, at which point, at the end of the Ice Age, the climate began to dry out, and that civilization thereafter remained extinct.

The sedimentary debris from the regional flooding originated in the surrounding high Andes which were then covered with perhaps several thousand feet more of Ice Age icepack, which then began to rapidly melt at the end of the Ice Age, causing widespread devastation, as it is noted by Hancock that:

> *Fragments of human and animal skeletons had been found lying in chaotic disorder among wrought stones, utensils, tools and an endless variety of other things. All of this has been moved, broken and accumulated in a confused heap. Anyone who would dig a trench here two meters deep could not deny that the destructive force of water, in combination with brusque movements of the earth, must have accumulated those different kinds of bones, mixing them with pottery, jewels, tools and utensils…Layers of alluvium cover the whole field of the ruins and lacustrine sand mixed with shells from Titicaca, decomposed feldspar and volcanic ashes have accumulated in the places surrounded by (ruins of megalithic) walls…*

Ice Age animals like the toxodon (which is a type of hippo), the so-called wooly mammoth, and the three-toed horse, according to Arthur Posnansky, were etched on megalithic monuments and pottery at Tiahuanaco, and even a big statue of the hippo-like toxodon was found, all of which allegedly died-out eight-thousand years earlier (at 10000 B.C.) than those temple complexes of Tiahuanaco were evidently constructed at around 2000 B.C.

Hancock has concurred with the 10000 B.C. date for the end of the Ice Age in portions of his writings, and in other portions, he attempts to tortuously fudge-forward the end of the Ice Age, and therewith, the extinction date of these types of animals, to around 6000 B.C., as to elastically and against all the evidence overlap his torturously back-dated time for megalithic building to 7000 B.C.

Mainstream archaeologists say that Tiahuanaco and the other great ancient megalithic sites in the Andes were built at least eight thousand years after the end of the Ice Age, when that region had allegedly been dry and desolate for those eight thousand years. But the evidence plainly indicates this religious ceremonial center and major trading hub for that region of Lake Titicaca was laid-waste by a destructive surge of Ice Age melt-water that may have varied in intensity through several decades when the Ice Age ice-pack melted over a period of decades circa 1500 B.C., a date which jibes with the advanced masonry and engineering of the megalithic structures which greatly resemble the other Lapita culture structures which dot the Pacific islands, all the way to those Andes.

Orthodox archaeologists say that the Lapita people from southern and eastern Asia navigated and settled the islands of the Pacific in crude boats with stone age navigational skills, such as knowledge of general directions by the sun and the wet finger stuck in the wind routine, so they would have us believe that the precise masonry work exhibited with the ancient megalithic walls, statues, pyramids, multi-level ceremonial platforms, and altars is the work of crude stone-age tribes who decided to set out across the seemingly limitless expanses of the Pacific in crude sailing vessels to sculpt from stone these sophisticated astronomically-related megalithic complexes which dot the islands all the way to the Andes.

As we proceed with this analysis of ancient history, you can see that these inconsistencies and contradictions of the orthodox timeline for ancient history are profuse and profound, yet these inconsistencies and contradictions are rarely allowed the light of day because satisfactory answers will obviously not be in the offing by mainstream archaeologists, so under the rug go these glaring contradictions of the orthodox timeline for ancient history.

Literally hundreds of Lapita megalithic building sites are scattered throughout the islands of the Pacific, from the Hawaiian Islands to New Guinea, and from the Ryukyu islands of Japan to the Fiji islands, and on to Easter Island, then even on to the Andes of South America. The Lapita people were metal-workers and masons extraordinaire, who exhibited skills which have since been lost for thousands of years from that time when the Lapita were precession-navigating, mining, smelting ore for metal-works, and carving and placing megalithic blocks for ceremonial courts, tiered-plazas, step-pyramids, and stone-circles which reflect anything but the supposed stone-age status of those sophisticated ancient seafaring-settlers of the Pacific.

Professor W. J. Perry in his 1923 book *The Children of the Sun*[19] documented the hundreds of megalithic sites throughout Indonesia and Polynesia, and he also noted the many megalithic sites of India, which are of the forms and functions like those found far to the east in the islands of the Pacific. I highly recommend this book because therein are records from Pacific island explorers and adventurers in India which describe the hundreds of megalithic sites (many of which have been since eliminated for modern development) in great detail from that time, a century ago, when the ruins were undoubtedly in a much more pristine state.

Perry goes into great detail about the forms and functions of these megalithic constructions which he correctly deduces are from an ancient culture of ore-smelting and navigationally sophisticated people who, according to the archaeological evidence, sailed and settled eastward from the Persian Gulf (from the cradle of civilization in the Middle East), to India, Indonesia, and Japan (Sundaland, or Mu), and on to the islands across the Pacific, all the way to the Andes of South America.

He also correctly states that these were a people of sun worshippers, who navigated by the stars, but Perry couldn't say how they accomplished this, and no one has been able to explain how these ancient, and supposedly stone age, transoceanic voyagers executed such precise navigation across thousands of miles of open ocean until we have understood that they were navigating by the stars, and very precisely by those, because they could measure the rate of precession with the archaeometer, and thusly, they could measure the earth, according to the hexagon of the circle of the earth, and thereby, they could chart the earth, and so, have the confidence from their technical savvy to sail off into uncharted seas, in search of mineral-rich lands for the smelting of the tools needed to construct their formidable structures of megalithic masonry, and to have the confidence that they would know from where they had come.

Captain Cook, who explored the Pacific in the 1700's, wrote the following description cited in Perry's book of a megalithic structure on the island of Raiatea near Tahiti:

> *It is a long square stonework built pyramidically; its base is 267 ft. by 67 ft.; at the top it is 250 ft. by (a mere) 8 ft. It is built in the same manner as we do steps leading up to a sundial or fountain erected in the middle of a square, where there is a flight of steps on each side. In this building there are eleven of such steps; each step is about 4 ft. 7 in., but they decreased both in height and breadth from the bottom to the top… The outside was faced partly with hewn stones and partly with others, and these were placed in such a manner as to look very agreeable to the eye. Some of the hewn stones were 4 ft. 7 in. by 2 ft. 4 in., and 15 in. thick, and had been squared and polished with some sort of an edge tool.*[20]

This structure is essentially a step-pyramid like so many others from ancient Egypt, Babylon, India, the Olmecs of Central

America, and from the Lapita culture of the Pacific which extended its megalithic sun-worshipping civilization all the way to the Andes of South America. These were an ancient people from the time when the Egyptians were building their first and by-far their most advanced pyramids, whose building would shortly thereafter reflect a rapid deterioration in engineering and masonry skills.

The same can be said of the Lapita people who spread east across the Pacific to South America to build the great megalithic complexes in the Andes, as they also had this high level of astronomical, metallurgical, and engineering acumen which apparently also seemingly came out of nowhere, and which also rapidly declined, apparently within about a thousand years. The most ancient tribes who still inhabit these regions have no idea how their ancestors built those impressive megalithic complexes which cannot be duplicated today with the current indigenous technical know-how. Their distant ancestors were different, they were engineers and surveyors with astronomical measuring savvy which was long ago forgotten.

The very first settlers in the various regions of the world who founded the earliest ancient cultures were the most technically advanced of all the people of those cultures ever since their earliest times, how ironic is that? This is the reverse of the orthodox dogma that technology and culture evolve over time into more complex forms. What we actually see is the degradation and loss of the advanced knowledge and skills demonstrated by these people-groups' earliest ancestors within a matter of centuries, and such is the last thing which orthodox science would predict.

On an island near Tonga in the south Pacific is a huge megalithic trilithon which is a pi-sign-shaped archway of two tall upright blocks capped with a connecting horizontal block called the lintel.[21] This trilithon has been described as like the trilithons of Stonehenge in England, and like those at other astronomically relevant megalithic stone-circles and temples found all across Europe, Asia, and others of the Pacific islands.

The Ice Age navigators obviously set-out to aggressively chart and settle the globe, and they were equipped to do so as they had marvelous astronomically-based surveying capabilities and technically advanced construction expertise which manifested in their prolific megalithic building in disparate locations of the world.

And because these structures worldwide are of similar forms and functions, and because the navigation skills required to venture out onto the vast uncharted seas are evidenced with the maps of the ancient sea kings, it does seem that the ancient settlers were radiating out from a region where is the site on the ancient Prime Meridian, the Great Pyramid of Giza, there near the Middle East, the "cradle of civilization."

10
CHAPTER

Sea Kings Settled Ice Age Europe

During the Ice Age, a vast snow and icepack, up to two miles deep, covered all of northern Europe (except the coastal areas), enveloping the Alps, and topped the highlands of the British Isles, when the Canaanites were navigating and settling far-flung areas of the globe, often where they found tin and copper deposits. Britain was such a target for the Canaanite (Phoenician) maritime profiteers, and they set-up shop there to mine, smelt, and farm at around 2000 B.C., as is acknowledged by many mainstream archaeologists.[1]

And as we have seen, these precession-measuring Phoenicians revealed their knowledge of precession with their stone-circles, temples, and courtyards, of motifs which embody precession, relating to the slow apparent movement of the wheel of the zodiac around the so-called World Tree, which is the earth's axis that would wobble once in 25,920 years.

With the archaeometer, the precession measurements were made, and the universal base six precession numbers such as 6, 12, 36, 54, 72, 108, and 432 fell out (so to speak), from the application of the measured rate of the slow apparent movement of the constellations along the horizon to the hexagon of the circle of the earth, as it relates to the earth's radius, and thereby, to the earth's circumference, and so, the ancients were able to accurately chart "the arch of the sky and the round face of the earth."

The British Isles are dotted with the sites of megalithic stone-circles, which were evidently built by the Canaanites (the Phoenicians), according to the relics which have been found associated with them, such as Phoenician purple dye, tell-tale Phoenician glass beads, Canaanite weapons, and nearby Phoenician tin and copper mines.[2]

These ancient stone-circles are like those found in Lebanon, Israel, Egypt, Arabia, India, Japan, the islands of the Pacific, and elsewhere, so they all apparently were constructed by settlers who had migrated from the Middle East, the cradle of civilization, where was built the monument to the ancients' ability to measure the earth according to measurements of the stars, and through which runs the ancient Prime Meridian for precession measurement and mapping, the Great Pyramid of Giza.

Mainstream archaeologists will admit that the Phoenicians were sailing the high seas (though they might say always within sight of land), as far back as 2000 B.C., and they say that Stonehenge and the other megalithic structures of England were built around 2000 B.C., so the connection should logically be made that the megalithic stone-circle-making Phoenician navigators from Canaan are responsible for the early works (like the copper and tin mines, the smelting locations, and the Phoenician style purple-dye and artifacts[3]), as well as, for the building of the associated megalithic structures, such as Stonehenge.

But the orthodox archaeologists say that they don't know who built Stonehenge, or the huge dirt-covered six-stepped pyramid Silbury Hill which, underneath all the dirt, has a megalithic structure like the Zoser Pyramid in Egypt,[4] or the Newgrange megalithic complex in Ireland, or the stone-circle complex at Callanish, or the many other stone-circles of astronomical measuring import which are found over much of the British Isles, and which look like those in Lebanon and Israel, and North Africa, and France, and eastward to India, and the islands of the Pacific.

Canaanite stone-circles are not found in the highlands of the

British Isles for a variety of fairly obvious reasons, but one not so obvious reason is that the Ice Age icepack had buried the British highlands when the Phoenicians were navigating and settling disparate regions of the world circa 2000 B.C., including the coastal regions of Ice Age Europe, where they carried on mining, smelting, and shipping operations, and where they built their many religious ceremonial stone-circles and pyramids for the outposts' inhabitants' religious practices, and legend holds that submerged megaliths are to be found off the Isles of Scilly, off Cornwall, and in Cardigan Bay.

In fact, there is a complete dearth of stone-circles and pyramids in mountains of northern Europe, because of the Ice Age icepack, which had set-upon inland northern Europe, the Alps, and the highlands of the British Isles, until about 1500 B.C., when all but the snow in the high Alps melted away, leaving vast territories open for settlement by the various surrounding Ice Age tribes, such as the Goths, who were the Gutis of upper Mesopotamia[5], and the Teutonic tribes, who moved in from the east at the close of the Ice Age.

There are a few dolmens, which are burial caves built of megalithic blocks, in that region, but they were built after the Ice Age icepack had melted off Europe, when the sea level rose to submerge many of the megaliths worldwide that had been built during the Ice Age on the coastlines which were submerged when about 25 million square miles of land were engulfed by the rapidly rising sea level, which was caused by the melting of the Ice Age icepacks.

An early settler of the British Isles named Partholon navigated with a party of about a thousand settlers in thirty ships from the eastern Mediterranean to Ireland in 1485 B.C., where nine lakes and three rivers were noted in the new land, and with the arrival of a second group, some fifty years later, it was then noted that "many new lakes and rivers were bursting forth,"[6] but bursting forth from where?

Water "bursting forth" from the bowels of the earth would have been a volcanic steam-event which would have, no doubt, curtailed the settlement, and the anomalously great heat of the waters bursting forth would have logically been duly noted by those early settlers, so the water obviously came from somewhere else, from the prolific waters which surged from the massive icepacks in the British Highlands when they melted at around 1500 B.C., as the Ice Age ended.

During the Ice Age, the British Isles were part of a huge peninsula which attached to Europe at Holland and Germany. In other words, the English Channel and the southern part of the North Sea was then dry land, and when the sea level rose about one hundred feet (only that amount because of the isostatic rebound of the nearby underlying continental crust due to the loss of the Ice Age icepack-overburden), it left the British Isles as the remnant of the peninsula which once extended northwest from Europe.

A port of call for Partholon on his way to Ireland may have been the legendary Phoenician port city of Tartessos (Tarshish), which is now on the seafloor near Gibraltar, off the western coast of the southern tip of Spain, near Rota. It is interesting that submerged megalithic structures have recently been discovered there near Gibraltar, so we shall see if mainstream scientists publicize this discovery, and then try to explain how these were "actually" not submerged when the Ice Age melted.

The megalithic blocks are precisely-tooled for tightly fitted stone structures, so it will be interesting to see how orthodox archaeologists explain (if they should bother) why there are 2000 B.C. vintage megalithic-blocks on a seafloor which they say was submerged at around 10000 B.C., when they say that the Ice Age icepack melted. Or will they tell us that proto-cavemen from 10000 B.C. were actually then building megalithic structures of massive, precisely-hewn stone blocks, and so, that the Great Pyramid could also have been built that long ago, by "cavemen?" Don't hold your breath for much commentary from mainstreamers, unless their feet are held to the fire.

Offshore from the port cities of Rota and Chipiona (on the shallow seafloor near that coastline of the province of Cadiz) have been found, in water down to a hundred feet deep, megalithic stones-slabs, a giant mill-stone, megalithic pillars, and megalithic walls, which have been reported by local fisherman and divers for decades. Prominent university professors in Spain, led by investigator Georgeos Diaz-Montexano, are trying to bring these submerged megaliths to the attention of the mainstream academic community.

He notes in a correspondence which announces their findings that:

> *In Chipiona we've also been able to confirm the existence of several 'paving stones' and 'flagstones,' clearly man-made, found in various locations, between one and four kilometers off the coastline, on the way from the Guadalquivir estuary to near Rota. These 'paving stones' were part of various stretches of walls described by the divers who found them as 'city walls.' We've been able to confirm these 'paving stones' are real, are man-made, and are composed of granite, a type of rock which cannot be found near the Cadiz coast.*

It is fascinating to note that the Zeno Map of 1532 shows this coastline when sea level was lower and when there was no Guadalquivir river delta. The map shows the river, but not the fan-like delta which is now at the mouth of the river, because the precession-derived source maps of the Tyranean Sea Fish of Phoenicia were drawn during the Ice Age, in the earliest stages of the build-up of that river estuary/delta.

Notice also that the granite blocks must have been hauled a long distance because there are no granite deposits in that region of southern Spain. Multi ton megalithic granite blocks from many miles away do not mysteriously move into place on the seafloor as precisely-hewn building components of megalithic walls and temples. These must be the ancient ruins of the Phoenician port city of Tartessos which may have been a way-station during Partholon's voyages to Ireland, if not then submerging.

But according to Irish history, there were settlers already in that land when Partholon arrived around 1500 B.C, reputed to have been quite large (giant) first settlers of that region, who were known as the Fomorians. They were probably the stone-circle builders of Stonehenge, Callanish, and some of the hundreds of others around the British Isles, as the Irish history records that they were Hamites, and Canaan was a Hamite, who sired Sidon, the namesake of the ancient Phoenician port city of current-day Lebanon, the ancient land of the precession navigating Phoenicians of the seaports (such as Sidon and Yarmuta) of the land of Canaan.

The stone-circles of ancient Canaan in the Middle East have been compared to those of the British Isles like Stonehenge and Callanish, and as we have seen the historical record of Canaanites (Fomorians) in the British Isles, the link to their having built the great stone-circles of the British Isles is a logical one.

And remember that Phoenician artifacts have been found associated with these stone-circles, and Phoenicians (Canaanites) are commonly agreed to have been sailing the high seas circa 2000 B.C., so some of those were the Fomorians, who had sailed to the Ice Age peninsula of northwest Europe, which later became the remnant British Isles, after the sea level had risen at the close of the Ice Age circa 1500 B.C., when Partholon's party arrived, also from the eastern Mediterranean, to encounter the Fomorians, and to note that many new lakes and rivers were then "bursting forth," which must have been from the melting Ice Age icepack of the highlands.

Partholon is said to have been of Scythian stock, whose ancestral homeland was upper Mesopotamia, but Partholon's clan had moved to Egypt sometime before 1500 B.C., developed a following, and then set off to settle their new land, a couple of thousand miles to the northwest in the eastern Atlantic. Because the Egyptians were demonstrably precession-navigators and surveyors, they had the where-with-all to voyage across the high seas, and as Partholon had probably dealt with the nearby trade-crazy sailing Phoenicians, their seagoing vessels would have also been available to Partholon, for the right price, of course.

The Phoenicians had, at that time, long since navigated into the Atlantic, the evidence being the presence of Fomorians (Canaanites) in Ireland when Partholon arrived there at around 1500 B.C., and the submerged Phoenician ruins of Tartessos on the shallow seafloor off the southwestern coast of Spain, which must have been built before the end of the Ice Age, because almost all agree that they were engulfed when the sea level rose due to of the melting of the Ice Age icepack.

The question is, did the Ice Age really end at around 10000 B.C., as is popularly advertised, and so, the megalithic city of Tartessos, noted in ancient lore, was actually built before circa 10000 B.C., when cavemen had supposedly just exited their caves to figure-out how to stick seeds in the ground and build wooden-ribbed animal-skin tubs in which to "navigate?"

Once again, you can see why mainstream scientists are reluctant to investigate the many submerged megaliths of the various ancient cultures. It is because the implications for their timeline for the Ice Age are made dire, after all, they must provide the answer to: did so-called cavemen actually build those megalithic complexes, or did the Ice Age really end much later than the popularly advertised date of circa 10000 B.C.?

And if they should choose to go with Hancock and Schoch that the Ice Age supposedly ended at around 6000 B.C., after those now submerged megaliths had been built, then they would be faced with the daunting task of explaining 4,000 years of missing ancient civilizations' histories, from 7000 B.C., up to about 3000 B.C. (their time), when the kings' lists of Berosus (from Babylon) and Manetho (from Egypt) begin, and the daunting task of explaining why they were off by about 4,000 years (from 10000 B.C. to 6000 B.C.) regarding the time for the end of the Ice Age. Those submerged megaliths cannot be explained away without dealing with the true and obviously later-than-advertised date for the end of the Ice Age at about 1500 B.C., after those now submerged circa 2000 B.C. vintage megaliths had been built.

The precession-measuring Canaanites who built astronomically-relevant stone-circles in the land of Canaan, as well as in Britain, and elsewhere, were evidently the first builders of such in Ice Age Britain, and Stonehenge, which is acknowledged to have been built around 2000 B.C., is of those the most famous. Stonehenge has been compared to the Canaanite stone-circles in the Middle East, so the link is quite plain, because I have demonstrated that the Phoenicians (Canaanites) were great precession measurers/navigators as evidenced with the maps of the Tyranean Sea Fish.

Dr. Gerald S. Hawkins charted with computer models the precession-measuring purpose behind the placement of the megaliths at Stonehenge, and his studies led him to deduce that by extrapolating back-in-time the positions of the constellations of the zodiac on the horizon at dawn at the summer solstice, the ancients built that facility with those positions for the megaliths at around 1500 B.C., and were measuring precession therewith at that observatory.

The Greek historian Hecataeus (circa 500 B.C.) was quoted by the Greek Herodotus (circa 50 B.C.) as saying that the Greeks traveled to an island "not smaller than Sicily" to worship the sun god Apollo every 19 years. This island was known as the land of the Hyperboreans because it is from where the north wind (the boreas) seems to originate. Arctic cold fronts blow from the northwest toward Greece, so this land was to the northwest of Greece, where is Britain.

It was said that the sun god Apollo visited the island of the Hyperboreans every 19 years, "the period in which the return of the stars to the same place in the heavens is accomplished." Obviously, Hecataeus at around 500 B.C. was speaking of the precession of the constellations, as the stars return to their same place in the heavens, which would in reality happen every 25,920 years, not every 19 years, so Hecataeus apparently was not quite up to speed on precession measurements, and was actually referring to the Metonic cycle (when the sun and moon return to their original relative positions in the sky every 18.6 years).

But the fact remains that those ancient Greeks of circa 500 B.C. sailed to Britain to a "notable temple which is adorned with votive offerings and is spherical in shape." Spherical in shape speaks of the great Stonehenge, and the fact that it was known as far away as Greece confirms the reverence which the ancients bestowed upon it, as many people do today. In fact, ancient Mycenaean (Greek) writing has been found on the megaliths of Stonehenge.

These massive trilithon megaliths of Stonehenge, for solar and lunar measurements, are surrounded by an outer ring of 56 Aubrey holes, which is a seemingly strange number of holes for a precession measuring installation, until we consider that a 3 hole move of a megalithic marker, representing the "big hand" of this precession clock, would designate 19 years (a Metonic cycle), as 19 x 19 equals 361, which is 1 more than the precession number 360, and after these 19 three-hole-moves of the "big hand" around the ring of Aubrey holes were completed, after 361 years, the marker-stone was then in the hole one past the 56th Aubrey hole, as 3 x 19 = 57, and it was at that point that the marker-stone became both the big and little hand of the precession clock, because it then marked 361 years, marked by the "big hand," and so, being 1 hole past 56, it simultaneously marked that completed block of years by showing 1 hole move of the "little hand" of that precession clock, with that same marker-stone move.

Then, after a second cycle around the Aubrey hole ring of the "big hand," the marker-stone would then have been 2 holes past "straight-up 56," so 2 x 360 then equaled 720 years of precession measurements, therefore, you can see that after 72 cycles of the marker-stone around the Aubrey ring, the marker-stone would then mark 72 x 360 = 25,920 years (the amount of time required for the earth's axis to wobble once, like a gyroscope in space, manifesting as the apparent slow movement of the constellations along the horizon, which causes the sun to move into a new zodiac "house" every 2,160 years).

In other words, the marker-stone completed a cycle one hole further around the circle of Aubrey holes than did the previous cycle(s), so after still another 361 years of precession measurements, the cycle completed one hole still further around, and therewith, also marked one hole still further around of the "little hand" which marked 360 year periods of time, but went one hole past the previous hole for the completion of this big hand cycle, and thusly and simultaneously, marked one more period of 360 years with the little hand, both being marked with the one marker-stone.

So you can see that the ancient Greek historian Hecataeus was accurately reporting the once per 19 year pilgrimages by the ancient Greeks to Britain, but not for his reported reason that after 19 years the constellations had returned again to their original positions, but because the 19 years marked yet another movement of the marker-stone for precession measurements. He had it half right since he knew that the pilgrimage was for the reverence of the movements of the houses for their sun god, Apollo, but the 19 years were of "big hand" ceremonial movements of the Metonic cycle, not of a 72 hole count of the "little hand" movements which would have marked the 25,920 years which it would have taken for the constellations to appear to move along the horizon one full 360 degree cycle because of the slow wobble of the earth's axis.

The precession-measuring megalithic structures such as Stonehenge are found in Europe, North Africa, the Middle East, India, and the Far East, some of which are now on the seafloor, because they were submerged when the Ice Age icepack melted, so it is apparent that the precession-measuring and mapping ancients of the Ice Age were then indeed navigating and settling much of the world, leaving behind as evidence of their exploits the precession-derived maps, the stone-circles, and the monument to their precession-measuring prowess, the Great Pyramid of Giza in Egypt.

11
CHAPTER

Base Six Games of the Ancients

Roll the dice, and then 1 of 36 possible combinations will come up because the 6 sides of one of the dice times the 6 sides of the other dice equals 36. Sounds familiar, doesn't it? Think of all the board games which we play, and you will see that base six numbering, rather than the modern base ten numbering, actually under-girds the counting systems of many of these games.

Base six numbering predominates in the ancient dice and board games, and this is not surprising, as we have seen that the six-sided polygon is the fundamental basis of the ancient precession-mapping system, because the ancients measured the hexagon (a six-sided polygon) of the circle of the earth through measurements, with the archaeometer, of the slow apparent movement of the constellations along the horizon.

The ancient Middle Eastern board game backgammon (which is virtually the nationals' sport) is based upon the hexagon of the circle of the earth, which we have also seen in the architectures and legends of these ancient people-groups. The backgammon board is four sections with six spaces per section for a total of twenty-four spaces, the same number as hours of the day. Two dice are used for play, so we see that the base-six methodology permeates the essence of this very ancient game.

Why the precession-derived twenty-four hour day, rather than what also could have been a precession-derived day of 12 subdivisions, or a day of 48 subdivisions, is a mystery, but the fact remains that the ancient (and there-from modern) timekeeping system is based upon the measurement of the movement of the constellations along the horizon because of precession, nothing more, and nothing less, as we have seen. Hour glasses (measuring 1/24th of a day) have predominated since ancient times, so that block of time was selected rather than the other options just mentioned.

Therefore, the ancient hour glass and the twenty-four-space backgammon game are obviously both from the precession-measuring Ice Age navigators, who were measuring the earth and incorporating their knowledge for their leisure activities like the board games at around 2000 B.C., when the great ancient cultures are commonly thought to have been flourishing, unless of course, you are trying to torturously back-date the ancient civilizations to around 7000 B.C., as to overlap a torturously moved-up date for the end of the Ice Age to around 6000 B.C., and so, to rationalize the presence of the submerged megalithic structures on the seafloor, which were engulfed when the Ice Age icepack melted, causing the sea level to rise a few hundred feet and cover about 25 million square miles of land.

The ancient Egyptians played two board games, Senet and Mancela, which are also base six denominated, as Mancela entails six moves with the victory coming on the seventh move, and the Senet board game entails thirty positions, which is also a base six derived number of operative positions, so orthodox archaeologists, equipped with their pop notions about ancient history, are clueless regarding the origin of the base six methodology of these games.

The orthodox archaeological notion is that the ancient Egyptians were ignorant of this base six methodology for mapping and timekeeping, but if that were true, one would think that the ancients would have gone with base five games rather than base six, after-all, there are five fingers to the hand, so one would logically deduce that the supposedly precession-ignorant ancient Egyptians, who were purportedly just learning how to build-up out from their supposedly caveman-like "evolutionary" existence, would have naturally gone with a simple and obvious system like counting their fingers and toes.

But no, we actually see base six methodology in the ancient leisure games of the supposedly caveman-like earliest builders of the great ancient civilizations, so how can this be, why not base five, like the number of fingers and toes on each appendage, or base ten, like the combined number of fingers or toes, or like base twenty, the combined number of fingers and toes? It is self-evident that finger and toe counting were not germane to the base-six methodology of these games, so according to the orthodox archaeologists, this base six methodology was selected merely out of thin air, for no apparent reason.

Speaking of the ancient Egyptians, did you ever wonder why the system for hat sizes? Please refer again to Appendix 1 to see that the value for pi was conveniently expressed by the ancients as 22/7. It is no coincidence that a typical hat size is 7, and this is because hat sizes were measured by the ancients using a standardized knotted rope which was wrapped around one's head, and the number of knots of that head-circumference was divided by pi (3.14) to result in the hat size.

Since the average head size is about 22 inches (size 7 hat), and since we don't call that average hat size a 22, we call it a 7, you can see that the hat measuring system was derived from the ancient knowledge of the value for Pi, as deduced from their precession knowledge and from their related knowledge that the length of one side of a hexagon is the same length as is the length of the radius of the circle which circumscribes said hexagon.

So your hat size is actually the averaged diameter of your head, because the circumference-length of your head, divided by Pi, equals the average diameter-length of your head. The ancients could have much more easily used the simple measured circumferences of heads for hat sizes, but no, they felt compelled to integrate their knowledge of precession and the related geometry into their hat-measuring methodology, and into their board game methodologies.

Ancient game boards were recently discovered in Iran which demonstrates that the ancient Elamites and Babylonians were also utilizing the geometry of precession mapping for their leisure activities, in addition to their architectural designs and astrological studies, like the ancient Egyptians, and others, as we shall see.

The ancient game boards, discovered near Jiroft in Iran, are shaped like an eagle or a human-headed scorpion, with 12 or 18 playing-holes on those boards,[1] so once again, base six methodology here, but not base five, or ten, or twenty from the finger and/or toe counting which orthodox archaeologists would predict from those ancient and purportedly geometry-ignorant proto-cavemen who supposedly had just crawled out of their caves to build the magnificent ancient megalithic structures with precession-derived dimensions and designs that we find in various parts of the world, both on land and now seafloor.

At the ancient Indus-Sarasvati civilization city of Mohenjo-Daro in northwest India have been discovered ancient dice which were finely crafted from clay or stone of superior workmanship.[2] Those ancients of that great Ice Age civilization, of which some of their vast building complexes are now on the seafloor because the sea level rose at the end of the Ice Age, as discussed in Chapter 1, had a highly sophisticated society of metal-smelters, farmers, livestock-operators, craftsmen, and precession-navigators, who passed some of their leisure-time playing games involving the base six dice, and finely-hewn stone game boards, which have been found were probably used with the dice for gaming.

Throwing the base six dice was also an ancient traditional leisure-activity in China, Central America, and Europe, so we must ask, why the universality of the six-sided cube, rather than a five-sided pyramidal dice, or an eight-sided octahedronal dice, or a ten-sided tetrahedronal dice?

With the widespread pyramid building in many parts of the world during the Ice Age, one might expect that the ancients would have memorialized their pyramid building with a five sided pyramidal dice, which would have also reflected the alleged primitiveness of the math capabilities of those ancients, who the orthodox archaeologists would surmise to have used the five or ten finger or toe count to measure the Great Pyramid of Giza, which actually, as we have seen, was designed with precession measurements and base six hexagon geometry of the circle of the earth.

But no, ancient base six game boards and dice are the rule, as in the ancient game of Chinese Checkers, the game-board of which is a hexagram (six-pointed star) with ten peg-holes per one (of the six) portions of the hexagram, for a total of sixty peg-holes for that ancient game board. The six-pointed star, sixty peg-holes, and six-sided dice, all are indicative of the precession-measuring basis for this and the other ancient games, there are no two ways about it.

12
CHAPTER

Human-Fish Demi-Gods of the Ancients

The ancient Ice Age cultures had common historical notions about a great global deluge which was survived by a remnant who were represented as human-fish demigods, and who were the early founders of those respective civilizations. The commonality of these legends, and the plainly described global nature of that deluge, defy the feeble rationales of obfuscation by mainstream academicians that the deluge was a figment of the ancients' imaginations, or that the legends actually merely describe local floods.

Over 500 people-groups today from six continents have this shared knowledge of the Deluge that was passed down from their earliest ancient ancestors,[1] so it is evident that the now extinct Ice Age cultures, from which derived many of the current-day tribes and cultures, were describing that same Deluge which is plainly portrayed to have been of Biblical proportions.

The famous Babylonian Epic of Gilgamesh, written around 2000 B.C., reports this cataclysmic global event which was survived by Utnapishtim and the Seven Apkallu[2] (Apkallu may be the root for the term apocalypse), and the ancient Hindus relate that Manu and the Seven Rishis survived this catastrophic global deluge, which was supposedly the most recent global cataclysm of a series of pralayas (cataclysms of water or of fire) that purportedly occur after yugas of time, which are multiples of the precession-derived number of 432,000 years.

It is plainly suspect that global cataclysms would predictably occur after a strict precession-derived number of years, as proponed by the Hindus, and the evidence from the geological record does not indicate multiple cataclysms of fire and water, so the Hindu notions about earth history are obviously grounded merely in their ancient precession-measuring capability, as all would agree that humans were not around to witness cataclysms which supposedly occurred after periods of time which are multiples of 432,000 years.

Note that the ancient Hindus also have legends of a limited rise of sea level which occurred within decades, as delineated in Chapter 1, so the flood of Manu with the Seven Rishis, that covered the entire globe, cannot be the same event mentioned in the Vedic stories from the Indus-Sarasvati region of circa 1500 B.C., that the sea level rose to cover the ancient city of Dwarka, the city which previously had been about fifty miles inland, nor can it be the same legendary (but limited) sea level rise described by the Tamil/Dravidians of southern India, when the ancient kingdom of Kumari Kandam was submerged, and those ancients then were forced to migrate a short distance to the north, as the sea level rose about three feet per year for about a century.

The Tamil/Dravidians of southern India had a different name for Manu, the hero of the global flood, which obviously preceded the later and limited sea level rise that occurred circa 1500 B.C. when the Ice Age ended. Their name for the global flood hero was Satyavrata, and he is said to have had three sons Sharma (Shem), Charma (Ham), and Japeti (Japheth),[3] so here is an independent corroboration of the Hebrew account of Noah's Flood, with the male survivors of that global flood being noted in that Hindu legend. Some call this just a strange coincidence, and if it were just a coincidence, I agree that it would be strange.

Notice Charma, the Ham of the Bible, his name is widely spread in many parts of the world, and he is the namesake of the

Chem in chemistry, and the charm of Charma (charms) has been associated with amulets to this day. He was known as the Sea Dragon to the ancient Montagnards of Cambodia (or Chambodia), and that ancient land was known as the Land of Champa (Hampa).[4] Ruins of an ancient megalithic city in southern India, Hampi, remain to reveal the impressive rock-hewn polygon block walls of those ancient Tamil/Dravidians, which greatly resemble those at the Valley Temple in Egypt and the megalithic walls in the Andes, and ancient Egypt was called Khem or Khemit, also known as the Land of Ham (Cham).

The Babylonian historian Berosus of circa 300 B.C. wrote that the global flood described in the epic of Gilgamesh occurred after 432,000 years of pre-Deluge kings' reigns,[5] so once again, we see this ancient notion of an impossibly long period of time for humans to have been counting years, and we see again that number, which was supposedly begun to be counted by humans that long ago just happened to turn out to be 10 times the number 43,200, which is the factor that the earth's dimensions were reduced by the ancients to establish the dimensions for the Great Pyramid of Giza, the monument to their earth-measuring capabilities, and the base reference point for the precession mapping carried-out by the Tyranean Sea Fish, among others.

Berosus wrote that Oannes and the Seven Sages endured the global Deluge, and these survivors of the Deluge were depicted as being part-human and part-fish, and they were known to have been great astronomers, mathematicians, and builders,[6] so apparently, these and the Tyranean Sea Fish were of the same group of early post-Deluge mariners who were mapping and navigating the globe during the Ice Age, which immediately followed the Deluge.

The cause of the Ice Age has been a great mystery to mainstream scientists, not because there isn't a rational explanation for it, but because they refuse to integrate common knowledge about the hydrologic cycle into their considerations, due to the fact that the implications of such an integration would be dire for their notions about earth history. It is strange that they don't consider the obvious, but the obvious impugns their timeline of earth history, so theirs is an oversight, not of ignorance, but of expedience, which we have seen is all too prevalent within the machinations of the ivory-tower types to jealously guard their mostly baseless notions about earth and human history.

Think about the atmospheric conditions during the Ice Age, a time of "black rain and constant twilight," as described in the pre-Mayan book *Popol Vuh*. Dense cloud-cover enveloped the earth during the Ice Age to produce the intense rain and constant twilight in the middle latitudes, such as in Central America, and to produce the intense snow blitz in the extreme latitudes, and there is only one mechanism which produces cloud-cover, and that single mechanism is the evaporation of water off bodies of water to ascend and form rain and snow clouds.

So obviously, and much to the chagrin of mainstream scientists, the evaporation rates off of the oceans of the world must have been much greater during the Ice Age. You can't explain the Ice Age, as has been badly attempted by mainstream scientists, through the integration of the so-called Milankovich Cycle, because that mechanism would not induce the much greater rates of evaporation required for the dense cloud-cover which obviously must have been the case to cause the Ice Age.

The Milankovich Cycle is the supposed slight change in the earth's orbit through one-hundred thousand year cycles that causes the earth to heat up and cool down through that cycle.[7] And the Ice Age occurred supposedly during a cool period of this cycle, but cooler air would cause less evaporation off of the oceans, the direct opposite of the conditions that actually are necessary for the Ice Age, so you can see that this theory for the causation of the Ice Age is specious because it is actually contradictory to the conditions needed for dense cloud-cover.

Most people assume that the Ice Age atmospheric temperatures were much colder than today, this is a common misconception which is fostered by mainstream scientists because they refuse to state the obvious fact that cooler atmospheric temperatures would cause less evaporation off of the oceans, which would then cause less cloud-cover, not more cloud-cover, for the Ice Age.[8] This is hydrology 101, but the mainstreamers expediently seem to forget the basic laws of hydrology because the implications are dire for their flimsy Darwinian scheme for the earth history timeline.

You now might be thinking, well then, according to hydrology 101, the atmosphere must have been paradoxically warmer during the Ice Age, to cause the much greater evaporation necessary for the formation of the dense cloud-cover. Warmer air temps would induce greater evaporation for more cloud-cover, but that cloud-cover then would cool down the atmosphere because the heat from the sun would be shielded by that cloud-cover, and so, cause the atmosphere to cool back down, therefore, the source of the heat for the warmer oceans must have come from below. This is discussed in my first book *Old Earth? Why Not!* I hope that you pick-up a copy to fill-out the puzzle from www.GenesisVeracity.com.

It should be fairly apparent from the legends about the Deluge that this cataclysmic event resulted in the warmer oceans to cause the Ice Age, and therefore, that the Ice Age ended when the ocean water had cooled to today's temperatures, such that the great evaporation rates necessitated for the dense cloud-cover for the Ice Age were no more, at around 1500 B.C., and so, the Ice Age icepack began to melt because the summers had become much warmer due to the disappearance of the dense cloud-cover which had caused cooler Ice Age summers, and which had caused warmer Ice Age winters because the clouds insulated the earth' surface environment.

Incidentally, the Deluge did not cover the current mountain ranges, as evidenced with the lack of radial tension cracks in the Deluge-caused, and now folded, sedimentary layers of the mountains, which indicates that the mountains actually rose at the close of the Deluge, while the sedimentary layers were still wet and soft, so that they didn't crack when tectonic forces caused the mountains to uplift with the associated folding of the sedimentary layers. (The cracks which do exist through sedimentary layers in mountains are called horsts or grabens, but they are extension features, having nothing to do with mountain-building, they occurred after the mountains had lithified, and are the result of fault-block dropping because of regional extension, not regional compression of the strata, as occurred with the mountain building.)

After that global cataclysm, the warmer ocean water for the greater evaporation to cause the dense cloud-cover of the Ice Age was in place, and it is then that the remnant survivors began to multiply, to navigate and settle much of the earth with their precession-mapping knowledge, which was obviously retained by the remnant through the Deluge, so the ancients began to build their megalithic structures of astronomical-measuring relevance with technology evidently not evolved from cavemen, but retained from the pre-Deluge world.

It is interesting to note that over 500 people-groups today from six continents have ancestral recollections of this global cataclysm, therefore, it is not surprising that all of the ancient civilizations also spoke of this cataclysmic event, through which the symbolically fish-like Oannes and the Seven Apkallu of Babylonia, Manu (Satyavrata) and the Seven Rishis of India, and Thoth and the Seven Sages of Egypt, survived to provide their progenies, the post-Flood civilizations, with the knowledge about astronomy, agriculture, and engineering, which only those surviving eight could teach (as obviously, the offspring of the eight knew not of the things pre-Deluge, as the offspring were born post-Deluge, and were in need of teaching).

This is why the Seven Sages of Egypt were known as the Builder Gods, they were the enlightened remnant who survived the supposedly precession-caused Deluge, as the Djed (World Tree) was supposedly shaken to cause the Bennu bird (the Phoenix) to purportedly rise, re-incarnated from the ashes of its own immolation, as a new world developed after the Deluge, the Deluge which is described in the ancient Egyptian Book of the Dead, considered to have been written circa 1500 B.C., and repeating the words of Thoth:

> *They have fought fights, they have upheld strifes, they have done evil, they have created hostilities, they have made slaughter, they have caused trouble and oppression... (Therefore) I am going to blot out everything which I have made. This earth shall enter into the watery abyss by means of a raging flood, and will become even as it was in primeval time.*[9]

Notice that here the speaking Thoth, also known as Tehudi (Tahiti?), which means measurer, is the creator of all, but not as one of the remnant eight through the Deluge, and this is typical of the murky picture regarding the gods' functions which are presented with the hieroglyphs and papyri from the ancient Egyptians, as other records indicate that Re or Atum was the creator god.

It is this cloudy overlap of functions which changed through time that renders a clear explanation of the ancient Egyptian pantheon impossible,[10] and the same can be said of the ancient Babylonian and Hindu pantheons, as they are also complex and overlapping in their respective members' functions, and thusly, these religious traditions are amalgams of precession science and real history, with the various gods playing varying roles in the supposed precession-marked evolution of history on the precession matrix which is symbolized by the World Tree, around which rotate the twelve constellations of the zodiac, like the spokes of a wheel.

It is interesting that the eight gods, the Khemenu of On (the City of the Sun, 15 miles northeast of Giza) in ancient Khemit (Egypt), who are said to have observed the creation of the sun[11] (and so, more blurring of the gods' functions), were also said to have been four pairs of male and female, that same breakdown as were of the eight who survived the Deluge, Noah (Manu), Ham (Khem of Khemit), Shem (or Sham), and Japheth (the Japeti of India, and the Iafeth of ancient Europe), and their four wives.

The Egyptians seem to have mixed the significance of the eight survivors (four male and four female) of the Deluge with a former time (the Zep Tepi, which means first time, or first mouth[12]), from when they mythologized those great earliest founders of the post-Deluge world as beings from the time of the creation, because the new post-Deluge world was like a new creation which had risen out of the water (the Deluge), like it did at the creation, because all the world looked new and different with its post-Flood mountain ranges which rose at the close of the Flood, and with the vast sedimentary layers with billions of creatures entombed therein (99% of which are marine creatures), stacked like pancakes to compose the new terra firma of the continents of the post-Deluge world, with its new hydrologic cycle caused by the warmer post-Deluge ocean waters which manifested the Ice Age.

Although Thoth is the hero of one Egyptian Deluge legend, there to the west of Giza is the mountain of Manu,[13] where the sun sets, and so to speak, where the sun (Osiris) dies, and therefore, symbolically, where the land of the dead is, where the dead of the Deluge are, the underworld, where the sun goes at night, only to be reborn in the morning as Horus, the son of Osiris. This is the life and death cycle of the sun, of the planting and harvesting cycle, and of the concept of resurrection by the ancients, but not resurrection as a spirit body, but as an astral projection, to become a star.[14]

Remember that the precession number 72 conspirators killed Osiris, then Isis put his body into a wooden chest (symbolizing Noah's Ark) and sent the chest off to the Temple of Baalbeck where is the architecture of base 6 significance, and where the legend says that the chest was grafted into the World Tree for his son Horus, the new sun, to come forth into a new age after a precession-caused cataclysm that shook the World Tree, after which the Builder Gods, the Sages, the architects of the Great Pyramid, navigated away from the Middle East, from the cradle of civilization, to map and settle much of the Ice Age world.

The Tyranean Sea Fish were probably so named because they were great navigators, and also because they were the same human-fish demigods as depicted in ancient Babylonian inscriptions, who survived the Deluge along with the hero Oannes, and Oannes was said to have gone under the sea at night (the setting sun), so apparently, the Deluge Noah was replaced with the notion that the sun brought mankind through the Deluge, not Noah, nor Manu, but Thoth, the Flood hero in one Egyptian legend, who was also said to have been the heart of Re (another name for the sun god). Corroboratively, the ancient Caananite god Dagon was a fish-garbed father of the sun god,[16] and the sun set, in Egypt, over the Mountain of Manu.

The relationship of the Flood hero to the sun god is further revealed with the Babylonian Flood hero named Ziasudra, presumably with the seven other fish-garbed demi-gods who sailed with the other-named Babylonian Flood hero, Oannes, who survived the Deluge with those seven fish-garbed family members, the Apkallu, the great builders and navigators of the post-Deluge world, who brought forth the knowledge which was prevalent in the pre-Deluge world, to be taught to their progeny born after the Deluge.

This hero Ziasudra sacrificed cattle and sheep to the sun god after the Deluge waters had assuaged,[17] showing further the ancient link of the Deluge to astronomical cycles, that is, linked to the sun entering a new "house," as occurred circa 2400 B.C. when the sun began to transition from its house in Taurus to its then new house in Aries. The other named hero from apparently the same event, Oannes, was depicted as a part-human part-fish demigod of great wisdom, who set at night like the sun, who rose like the sun the next morning, and to whom in the other legend, Ziasudra sacrificed as the sun god.

As the Phoenician (Canaanite) chief god Dagon was depicted as a fish-man whose son was said to be Baal the sun god, we can readily see the linkage to the Babylonian stories, and less readily to the Egyptian notions about Osiris and his reincarnation as Horus, the new sun of the morning, and the new sun, so to speak, which enters a new house every 2,160 years, when was expected a shaking of the World Tree to cause global cataclysm. Ancient astrologers expected a world shaking event some 2,160 years after the Deluge,[18] and as it turned out, the event was not geological, but was Spiritual, and but actually happened about two-hundred years after the sun's house changed to Pisces, it was the Incarnation of Jesus Christ, an event which surely shook the world, but not in a way which most of the precession-measuring astrologers were expecting, and which was about two-hundred years too late, according to their religion of precession.

In the Babylonian Epic of Gilgamesh, where the Flood hero Ziasudra survived the Deluge with his family onboard (plus representatives of the various kinds of animals), it was said that the goddess Ishtar viewed the whole watery cataclysm, and noted that the sea was glutted with bodies like fish. Here we see again the equation of fish representing men, and eight of these fish-like humans survived the mass drowning to become known as the first great builders and navigators in the then new post-Deluge world, when began the Ice Age which ended at around 1500 B.C. to cause sea level to rise and cover some of the great megalithic structures of those earliest post-Deluge settlers.

The Mechoacanesecs of central Mexico, who probably derived from the ancient Olmecs who had navigated from North Africa, spoke of the Deluge which left the new world littered with the bodies of the unsaved drowned people on which the vulture fed which had been released from the large vessel after it had it landed on a high mountain which had emerged from the Flood water.[19] The parallels to the Noah's Flood story are undeniable, and remember it is the rare people-group, both current and ancient, who did not have a legend similar to this one about the global Deluge.

If the Deluge actually did not happen, what are the odds that this huge variety of people-groups, both present and ancient, from six continents would have virtually the same legend about a difficult to imagine Flood which covered everything except the remnant humans and animals on the large vessel? Mainstream archaeologists rarely mention these widespread Global Flood legends for obvious reasons, for then they would be forced to explain how and why these clear accounts of a global catastrophe are supposedly just exaggerated versions of local flood accounts.

But these legends speak of a remnant of the humans and the animals, with all of the rest having died in the Deluge, so this relates that animals and humans could not have simply climbed a high hill to avoid the supposed (by mainstream archaeologists) to have been merely local flood, because there was nowhere to hide, as all of the earth was inundated. I hope that you look into my first book *Old Earth? Why Not!*, as it answers many of the geological questions which I'm sure did pop into your mind. The evidences are truly overwhelming that the earth and universe are actually much younger than is popularly advertised, and it all dovetails nicely with the material presented in this book.

The Hindu god Vishnu (whose symbol is the hexagram) is said to have incarnated as a huge fish which pulled the big ship of

Manu and the Seven Rishis that also carried all the kinds of animals and seeds to survive through the Deluge, to start a new yuga of time. Yugas are multiples of the precession-derived number 432,000 years that follow the supposed multiple prayalas (global cataclysms) of fire or water, and water caused the "most recent" pralaya of Manu and the Seven Rishis.

Remember that Manu was known as Satyavrata in southern India, and he was noted to have been the first teacher at the first Sangum (school) of the Kingdom of Kurmari Kandam, which is now on the shallow seafloor of extreme southeastern India, because it was submerged at the end of the Ice Age circa 1500 B.C., when the Pandiyan king Nediyon was forced to conquer territory to his north, as his previous kingdom was engulfed by the sea within a matter of decades.

Here we have the hero of the Deluge, Satyavrata (Manu), with his sons Sharma, Charma, and Japeti (and their wives) surviving the Deluge to help develop the earliest civilizations, like Kumari Kandam of the ancient Tamil/Dravidians, which is commonly considered to have been flourishing at around 2000 B.C., so you can see that the date for the Deluge is reasonably at around 2400 B.C., with the Tower of Babel incident circa 2200 B.C.

Michael J. Oard produced a study on the time necessary for the thermal dissipation off the warmer post-Deluge waters to cool the oceans to today's temperatures, and that thermal dissipation timeframe was calculated to have been about eight-hundred years, from about 2300 B.C. 'til 1500 B.C., when the oceans had cooled to today's extent, and then the high evaporation rates off of the oceans were no more to cause the dense cloud-cover which must have been the cause of the Ice Age.[20]

You may want to run the calculation yourself. The premise is that the post-Deluge waters were about 80 degrees F., and cooled to today's average ocean temperature of 50 degrees F., now just run the heat dissipation equations, and I'm sure you'll find that the dissipation rate caused the oceans to cool within about eight-hundred years. And remember, the only way to explain the Ice Age is because of paradoxically warmer oceans, there is no other rational explanation.

And please know that much of the timeline by orthodox archaeologists is hinged upon carbon 14 dating results, and as stated previously, those dates are notoriously unreliable, particularly those dates from organic material which lived during the Ice Age, when thousands of volcanoes were spewing carbon dioxide, containing carbon 12, into the atmosphere, which diluted (so to speak) the carbon 14 in the atmosphere, and therefore, the dates from the Ice Age have been determined from samples with too little carbon 14 relative to carbon 12, and this causes exaggerated carbon 14 dates.

Note that mainstream scientists wouldn't dream of considering carbon 12 dilution from thousands of volcanoes, because they consider artifacts of civilizations to be in the three to five thousand year old range, and they think that rampant volcanism was occurring about ten thousand years before that, when they think the Ice Age was at its peak, so they seem to ignore the large amount of volcanic ash within polar icepacks which is indicative of those volcanoes going off early and throughout the Ice Age, when much civilization was burgeoning, as we have seen.

The fish-man demigods of the Ice Age, allegorized by many ancient cultures, were the survivors of the Deluge, the ancients' earliest knowable ancestors, from whom all of the tribes and nations descended in the centuries after the Deluge, as they ventured out to navigate and settle fur-flung regions of the globe, with their precession-navigating skill, and their lust for gold, tin, and copper, and their knowledge that they could always go-back, because they could measure where on the earth they were, as they measured the movement of the stars relative to geographical locations, they could "measure the round face of the earth, and the arch of the sky."

13

CHAPTER

Neanderthal and Homo Erectus Were Us

Located generally within hundreds of miles of the areas of the world which were covered by the Ice Age icepacks are found bones of humans which have been imaginatively characterized as proto-humans, Neanderthal Man, and Homo Erectus, because these fossils show some insignificant morphological variations which have been explained as actually being merely anomalies of those ancients' life longevities and pathologies.

The remains of these supposedly subhuman ancients are found with their clothing, musical instruments, ritual burial ware, art work, and tools, yet we are expected to believe that they were somehow subhuman because of their thickened brow-ridges, or bowed-legs, or muscular builds, or because of stone tools that lead the orthodox scientists to have visions of a bouncing monkey-man who "just millions of years before" had been an evolving tree shrew, or some form of monkey, or whatever might be the human ancestor de jour.

Some humans today in fact work with "merely" stone tools, so for this reason, we are to believe that those among us who choose to live a simple life using stone tools are therefore subhuman? And what about all the evidence that those ancient and allegedly subhuman creatures were spiritual beings who buried their dead, created works of art, played musical instruments, and manufactured clothing? Are these the vocations of primitive monkey-men who ostensibly could barely count their fingers and toes?

In his landmark book *Bones of Contention*, educator Marvin L. Lubenow[2] presents an avalanche of compelling evidence that the minor physical variations of those ancient bones can be explained as caused by the great age at death of those people, or by their commonly suffered pathology, rickets, or by a combination of the two, which simply rationalize the slight variances of cranial dimensions and thickness of bones which we see in the so-called Neanderthal and Homo Erectus bones.

Much ancient literature describes that the earliest humans lived much longer than we do, back in the proverbial Golden Age of Mankind, so ancient history is on Lubenow's side, and the dense cloud-cover of the Ice Age did impede sunlight, which then impeded the manufacture of Vitamin D in humans, and so, helped cause the thickened brow-ridges and bowed-bones of some of the alleged proto-humans who undoubtedly lived a rugged existence in the Ice Age hinterlands of Europe and Asia, so Lubenow's cogent appraisal dovetails very nicely with the post-Deluge Ice Age conditions.

So-called Neanderthal bones have been found in shallower strata than "fully human" bones at an archaeological dig on Mount Carmel in Israel,[3] so from this we can see that "Neanderthals" lived there after did "humans," and showed the same technological expertise as did their "human" predecessors, who had shortly before lived there during the Ice Age from circa 2300 B.C. 'til 1500 B.C., when the great ancient megaliths were being built in that vicinity (Canaan), and in Egypt, Europe, Asia, and the Americas, when the Ice Age mariners ventured out to measure, map, and mine the earth and its resources.

Please refer to Appendix V for a viable model of our biological history which jibes with the evidences, and which frames the creation-evolution debate in a whole new light, rendering Darwinian theory as the plain, yet imaginative, charade that it is, and showing that the Darwinian term "species" is actually a meaningless subdivision of types of animals. The variations which we see within kinds of animals (like the cats or the horses) do reflect natural selection, so to speak, but not in a way such that cats and horses might one day evolve to fly, or evolve to read and write, as Darwinian theorists unbelievably deem plausible.

The rapid variation (natural selection), which was certainly biologically possible in the centuries after the Deluge, during the Ice Age, within the various animal kinds (like cats, or horses), is admitted by Hancock in his book *Underworld* to have happened with, in this case, the aid of the early settlers in the Indus-Sarasvati region at Mehrgarh, as they built and developed in that area, which then was lush and fruitful (but now is barren), where game like swamp-deer, gazelle, blackbuck, wild pig, and elephant abounded, and where was noted:

> *...a sequence of events that seems to document the local domestication of animals. The sheep, goats and cattle start out looking wild, and were manipulated... Over time the potential domesticates came to look like domesticated animals (smaller, with the osteological hallmarks of domesticated beasts).*[4]

Refer now, or later, to Appendix V to see how this all applies to the Global Flood Model (the GFM), which I obviously propone, and which allows the pieces of the puzzle of evidences from all the germane fields to effortlessly fall into place. This model seamlessly accommodates the evidences from biology, geology, anthropology, ancient history, and even astronomy, so I urge you to familiarize yourself with the legion of evidences which are necessarily ignored by the purveyors of orthodoxy, the orthodoxy whose model horribly accommodates the abundant pieces of evidence.

The ancient historian Eusebius recorded that the Greeks said that their civilization began 1313 years before the first Olympiad, and those Games began in 776 B.C., so you can see that the calculated date for the beginning of the Greece at 2089 B.C.[5] fits nicely within the GFM, as does so much other evidence. And one of the original events in the Olympics was the discus throw, so what was the origin of that strange and seemingly pointless athletic endeavor?

For years I have perused accounts about archaeological digs where were often found so-called hand-axes, and I always thought that hand-axes were just that, a rock axe-head which was affixed to a handle. But as it turns-out, those "hand-axes" are actually flat almond-shaped rocks, with a sharpened edge all the way around, that is, the "axe" blade goes all the way around those discus-like objects.

I have since learned that by "hand-axe," archaeologists mean a cutting rock-tool held in the hand, and not by a handle, but the chiseled edge going all the way around the discus-like rock does not make sense to have been a hand-held cutting tool, so because the thing flies like a discus, and ends up landing big-end-of-the-almond-shaped-rock-down, and on the "blade" portion, eight out of ten times, it seems that this was a hunting device.[6]

And as the rock "hand-axes" are almost invariably found where was water, where large animals once came to drink or to ford to the other side, it seems apparent that these rock tools were thrown like a discus at those large animals until they buckled under a barrage of those "hand-axes," at which point, they would be finished off with the spear. Here is a logical explanation for the origin of the discus event in the ancient Olympics that has a sound archaeological basis,[7] but would never be entertained by those of orthodoxy because "cavemen" and the ancient Olympics should have no interrelationship, whatsoever, according the orthodox dogma.

And these ancient discus-weapon specialists lived during the Ice Age, when Vitamin D-causing sunlight was relatively scarce, and when Vitamin D food sources like fish and eggs may have been scarce so that the pathological characteristics of rickets were manifested in their remains.[8] But from these few malformed bones of ancient humans, a supposed evolutionary connection has been projected back in time to proto-monkeys, or to tree shrews, or to some other such thing, it is a strange world, that world of Darwinian dogma.

Author Marvin L. Lubenow notes in his great book *Bones of Contention*[9] that so-called Homo Erectus, Neanderthal, and "fully human" remains have been discovered together, having had practiced the same skills as their brethren, and brothers they could well have been, if some had grown-up in a Vitamin D-deficient environment of little sunshine and no significant food sources of Vitamin D, to manifest as the morphological variations from "fully humans" noted in the remains of the so-called Neanderthal and Homo Erectus people.

There is the vast swath of shallow seafloor where Holland and Germany were connected to Britain during the Ice Age, where upon are now the relics of the "stone age" civilization called Doggerland. There is evidence of the so-called Ahrensburg people[10] there on the now submerged Dogger Banks, who manufactured "hand-axes" (nod, wink) and other stone tools, and who apparently lived the simple life far away from the megalithic religious centers such as Stonehenge, Callanish, and Carnac in France, which were being built then, during the Ice Age, by the precession navigators who were moving out from Canaan and Egypt, practicing their preoccupation with precession-measured navigation, and with the resultant religions of the Wheel of Time (they imagined that nature is affected by the sun moving into a new "house" every 2,160 years).

But the "stone age" people of Doggerland lived simply by hunting and fishing, living off the bounty of the land, and this was in fact during the Ice Age, when the warm post-Deluge ocean waters allowed a temperate climate along the coastlines of Ice Age Europe, as the massive Ice Age icepack up to two miles deep was accumulating on the continental interior of Europe (and on the highlands of Britain).

The climate along the ocean shorelines of Europe during the Ice Age was similar to that of London, lots of rain and clouds, but not much snow because of the proximity of the ocean which actually warms the atmosphere near the shoreline.

When the oceans were warmer during the approximately eight centuries after the Deluge, this coastal warming effect was even more pronounced, and therefore, although the icepack was building rapidly away from the ocean shorelines, the warmth of the water allowed a rainy and temperate environment for those rugged hunter/fishermen of Doggerland, and such was true of the Bering Land Bridge which connected Siberia to Alaska during the Ice Age, when the ancestors of the northwestern American tribes came across from Siberia to explore and settle new lands.

The tribes of the southwestern, southeastern, and north-eastern portions of the U.S., appear to have settled those regions from the south, from the land where the Olmecs landed from North Africa, to build their great precession-measuring megalithic civilization of sun worshippers. And there is evidence of the Lapita culture of the Pacific (who built the Andes megalithic cities) as far north as Baja,[11] so their influence on the earliest settlement of the now U.S. should not be discounted.

In his book *Children of the Sun*, author W. J. Perry details that the great mound (often terraced for crops) builders of the Mississippi, Tennessee, and Ohio river drainage systems had migrated up from Mexico to establish, near ore deposits, their earth and timber fortressed cities, mounds, and earthen-pyramids of astronomical relevance, and mound configurations characteristic of an astronomically-savvy people, so such is consistent with their migration up from the south,[12] from one of the two great sun-worshipping hubs of the Western World (the other in the Andes), up from the land of the sophisticated Olmecs of southern Mexico, who were the earliest people (along with the trans-Pacific Lapita of the Andes) to build pyramids and tiered-plazas in the Americas, and some tribes then ventured out from those regional hubs to rough it, relatively, in the ensuing centuries.

The tribes who walked across the Bering Land Bridge from Asia to North America during the Ice Age were mostly totem tribes who paid homage to their deities with their totem pole, a tree of ancestral beings, that may symbolize the ubiquitous World Tree and the god-like ancestors who survived through the last supposed shaking of it which caused the Deluge, the global flood of which many of these northwestern America tribes have ancestral recollections.

The tribes which descended from the ancient precession-measuring sun-worshippers of southern Mexico and the Andes, who came to their respective lands by sea, with the navigation and mapping expertise demonstrated with the astronomically-derived dimensions of the Great Pyramid of Giza (and not coincidently, with the dimensions of the Olmec's Pyramid of the Sun at Teotihuacan), these early tribes were attuned to the movements of the stars and sun.

And with the buried sea-going vessels at Giza, and with the maps of the ancient sea kings, and references of trans-oceanic voyages in the *Popol Vuh*, these navigating tribes were more astronomically-learned than were the tribes who came by land, across the Bering Land Bridge from Siberia during the Ice Age, and so, the navigating tribes' descendents, such as the Yuchi, the Natchez, and other mound builders, show ceremonial sun and star worship designs in their art and architectural alignments.

The Pyramid of the Sun at Teotihuacan in Mexico is part of a vast megalithic complex which is laid out much like Giza, with the three major pyramids configured like the three stars of Orion's Belt. This Orion is the Osiris of ancient Egyptian religion, who is said to resurrect when the sun rises in the morning, when that great life-giver comes back to life from the land of the dead, which is the night.[13]

And not coincidently, the perimeter length of the massive Pyramid of the Sun of the Olmecs (at Teotihuacan) is a precession-derived number, it is 4 times pi (3.14) times its height, whereas, the Great Pyramid is 2 times pi (3.14) times its height,[14] so the Pyramid of the Sun is a relatively flattened-out version, so to speak, of the Great Pyramid, and its astronomically-derived dimensions are as plain to see as those of the Great Pyramid (just a reduced height by a factor of two), and we know that the Olmecs had a base six precession-based calendar system, so the Olmecs, and the tribes which descended from them, had the precession-knowledge, but which quickly faded, as some of the descendants moved off to the north, to build the great tiered pyramids of the "mound builders" of the southeast U.S., but apparently lost their skill of precession mapping.

The ancient sun god of Olmec Mexico was Quetzacoatl (which means feathered serpent), and his feathered and serpentine character recalls that the Egyptian Horus (the pharoah), the new sun, the son of Osiris (god of the dead), was symbolized by the hawk, and the sign of wisdom which adorned the pharoah's crown was the serpent (cobra), so the reborn child of the sun (the then current pharoah) was wise as a serpent, and had an astral home which could be accessed like a bird can fly into the heavens.

The supposed wisdom from the astral realm came down from Draco, the Dragon, who is perched at the top of the World Tree, who never moves from there as the 12 constellations rotate around the mill of heaven, whose drive shaft (the World Tree) is topped by that wily and purportedly wise Dragon, who was to be feared and appeased by the ancients, thinking that their fate was determined by that supposed controller of the World Tree, who rests in it above, while the sun moves through 12 houses of the zodiac in 25,920 years of the slow wobble of the earth's axis, like a gyroscope in space, that causes the constellations of the zodiac to seem to move along the horizon at the rate of 72 years per 1 degree of 360 degrees.

Though the sun was seen by various ancient cultures as being the life-giver, who actually provided the breath of life when newborns first open their mouths, Draco (the Dragon) was the controller of the Wheel of Time, as all the other constellations seem to rotate around him, he was the hub who does not move, and so, he was seen as the one constant controlling factor, the director, who orchestrated the cosmic drama which supposedly proceeds further when the sun enters its new house after another 2,160 years.

The Quiche Mayans, who descended from the Olmecs, gave us the ancient history book the *Popol Vuh*, which describes the black rain and constant twilight of the Ice Age, and tells that the ancient ancestors sailed from the east (evidently from North Africa), when they could measure the round face of the earth and the arch of the sky (precession mapping). And from those ancient Olmecs derived the "stone age" tribes who had moved away from the Olmec homeland in southern Mexico, in search of more gold, tin, and copper, as well as, the fertile game-filled territories to the north, in the southern and eastern U.S., so the "stone age" builders of the sophisticated mound cities in the U.S. were of Olmec ancestry, but their skills degraded somewhat when they moved away from their early cultural and religious centers.

The so-called cavemen and stone age people of the Ice Age, when tribes were settling all over the globe, were those who ventured away from the first cultural centers, first away from the Mesopotamia and North Africa, and then away from outpost hubs, such as from the Olmec megalithic civilization centers at Palenque, Chichen Itza, and La Venta, and from the Lapita culture hubs of the Andes, from the Stonehenge-Canaanite culture hubs, from the Indus-Sarasvati and Tamil/Dravidian culture hubs of India, and from the Jomon civilization on the shores of northern Sundaland, all of whom had initially migrated from the cradle of civilization in the Middle East region at the beginning of the Ice Age.

The clans and tribes who ventured further than the major megalithic settlements were not crude cave-dwellers who could barely count their fingers and toes, they were in fact the offspring of those sophisticated precession navigators and megalithic engineers, but some of them moved away from those cultural learning centers, founded by their fathers, to live the simple life in remote locations, to live off the land, often without benefit of metal-smelting (though many of the early "stone age" migrants were in search of ore deposits in all parts of the world, to trade the ore, if not to smelt it).

Even mainstream archaeologists admit that an ancient maritime civilization extracted huge volumes of copper ore from the mountains of the Great Lakes region, and as the amount of copper needed to equip the vast armies and civilizations of the Middle East, beginning from circa 2000 B.C, far exceeded the mining opportunities in the Middle East, and as many evidences of a Phoenician presence in the Americas have been documented, it seems that those intrepid star-navigators were seeking new mining opportunities in the newly exposed terrain of the Great Lakes region which had been beneath thousands of feet of Ice Age icepack until about 1500 B.C., when the oceans had cooled to today's temperatures, and so, the evaporation for the dense cloud-cover of the Ice Age then dissipated.

In the mining region of northern Wisconsin is the lake known now as Rock Lake, but the native name for it is Lake Tyranena.[15] Ring a bell? The Tyranean Sea Fish were credited by the Turks of the 1500's A.D. to have been the authors of the maps which they compiled for their accurate maps of the Atlantic and Indian Oceans, and they were renowned for their far-flung monopolistic mining operations which were enabled by their superior knowledge about precession navigation, and by their statements to the navigationally ignorant like "don't sail too far lest you will fall off of the edge of the world, or you will be eaten by dreadful sea monsters."

The tribes of northern Wisconsin don't even know who extensively mined that area and left behind the artifacts of apparent Phoenician origin, and even a long rock pyramid which is beneath the waters of Lake Tyranena is almost beyond the tribal memories of the natives, but the name of the ancient miner/navigators who scoured that area for metal ore was retained with the legendary name of Lake Tyranena, derived from the name Tyre of a major port city of ancient Canaan, and so, the evidence is overwhelming that precession navigators had actually sailed all the way up the Mississippi River to access the bountiful mining opportunities in the newly exposed post-Ice Age Great Lakes region.

When the Phoenician mining operations ended in the Great Lakes region, perhaps at around 1000 B.C., as the Phoenicians were winding down their far-flung mineral exploitation operations with the beginning of the widespread use of iron (which was plentiful) in the Old World, when the Israelites had settled much of Canaan, after leaving Egypt a few centuries previously, to seriously infringe upon the Canaanites' (Phoenicians') wherewithal to operate as they had previously, at that time, no doubt, some of these ancient Phoenician settlers remained in their new and remote homeland in the Great Lakes region to intermarry with their distant cousins from North Africa, the Libyco-Berber speaking Olmecs, whose language shows a great affinity to the African Manding people of Libyco-Berber origins from the time when the Sahel of North Africa was a series of lakes and interconnecting rivers,[16] where the Manding people's Libyco-Berber-speaking ancestors flourished during the Ice Age, when just to the east was flourishing the civilization of the great Egyptian pyramid builders, and just to the northeast from there was flourishing the great star-worshipping megalithic culture of the Canaanites (the Phoenicians).

The ancient legend about the long rock-pyramid in Lake Tyranena in Wisconsin (that looks like those of the Teneriffe Islands near Tartessos at Gibralter) is that an ancient king flooded the pyramid so that his enemies would not take it from him. Though the manmade flooding may be an embellishment, the manmade nature of that anomaly on the lake-bed was known to the natives, and that was an area of demonstrably heavy Phoenician mining activity, so the ancient naming of the lake after the port city of Tyre in Canaan should not be big shocker, but it is truly a startling confirmation that those precession navigators were sailing just about everywhere from their home base in the Eastern Mediterranean (and from the Arabian Sea eastward to Sundaland and on across the Pacific).

The great mound building civilizations of the southern and eastern U.S., whose designs reveal good knowledge about astronomy, were developed by Olmec descendants from the south, who intermarried with the Phoenician pioneer remnant from the Great Lakes, and some of the Phoenician remnant, little doubt, intermarried with some of the totem tribes who had migrated across the Bering Land Bridge from the northwest down into the Americas, and so we see blue eyes in the Mandan of the central plains of the U.S., and a generally more Caucasian appearance of some of the northern plains and woodlands tribes, like the Sioux and the Fox tribes. Notice too that Mandan bears similarity to Mande, the people from whom the Olmecs derived of North Africa, when it (the Sahara) was lush and dominated by ten to twelve large lakes which were interconnected by river channels, when the precession navigators were building stone-circles in the region, like at Siwa and Nabta in the eastern Sahel (now Sahara).

Ancient mound cultures have also been discovered, east of the Andes in the jungles of the Amazon, and the layouts of those towns reveal advanced surveying skills which apparently were derived from astronomical measurements,[17] a skill that probably came from their ancestors over the mountains in Peru and Bolivia, the Lapita people, who had come across the Pacific with their precession-navigation and surveying prowess to build the awesome astronomically-aligned megalithic structures of the pre-Inca Andes culture, some of whom continued across the Andes into the Amazon, having some of their ancestors' technological savvy which was soon lost.

These have been described as "prehistoric early humans," but in reality, they were the earliest settlers in remote parts of the world, who gradually lost their ancestral knowledge about the precession rate of the constellations as it relates to geographical distances and surveying, when they also lost the seemingly hand-in-glove engineering savvy to build those fantastic structures of massive and precisely hewn blocks.

The so-called cavemen of "prehistoric times" were actually the progeny of the Sages, the Apkallu, the fish-like ancestors (memorialized as mermaids) who survived the Deluge, and then began the great precession-derived building and mapping projects of the post-Deluge, Ice Age era, and some of their offspring became "cavemen" as they moved off into the hinterlands to live off the land and make due with stone tools and whatever metal they may have produced.

The use of metals was reserved essentially for the affluent in those days, as processed iron was worth more than gold in ancient Egypt, and bronze had to be processed by smelting together copper and tin, so the hillbilly types (I can say that 'cause I'm from Oklahoma) made-due with the stone tools which they could easily manufacture, so-much for the so-called Stone Age of our "evolutionary ancestors."

To say that those "stone age" relatives of their more urbane, city-slicker, and metal-buying relatives, were actually evolutionary progenitors of those ancient city slickers is like saying that the "stone age" people of the jungles of New Guinea, or from the hills of Oklahoma today, are less evolved (in a Darwinian sense) than others who are more educated and technologically sophisticated. However, some people have always gotten-by with less, and that can actually be construed as a sign of greater intelligence.

14
CHAPTER

Supposed Astral Extensions to Mankind

With the survival of only eight humans through the Deluge, it is predictable that the progeny of this remnant developed different stories about their history as they moved away from the cradle of civilization, where the remnant disembarked in the mountains of Ararat of eastern Turkey at the close of the Deluge.

But it seems that most ancient cultures developed the notion that they were descended from the children of the sun, and they saw themselves as descended from such as the Egyptian Set of the underworld (as the sun "sets" at night), or from such as the Egyptian Horus, from whom the pharoahs were supposedly descended, as the dead pharoah, represented by Osiris, overcame the evil one known as Set (which means underworld[1]), the bringer of darkness at night, to resurrect as the son of Osiris, the risen sun Horus, who overcame the evil Set to bring forth light.

The brothers Osiris and Set were said to be children of the creator of all, the sun god Atum-Re, who was said to have self-created on the primordial mound,[2] which was the mountain in the pre-Deluge Garden of Eden, from which flowed the four great rivers mentioned in Genesis. The Great Pyramid is symbolic of the so-called primordial mound of the Zep Tepi, the First Time,[3] which the ancient Egyptians said was on the huge pre-Deluge island, confirmed by geology to have been the pre-Flood super-continent called Pangea, which broke apart (runaway plate tectonics) to form the continents of the post-Deluge world.

I cover the dynamics of the Deluge in great detail with my book *Old Earth? Why Not!*, but a brief and interesting note here, which is one proof of the rapid deposition of sediments on the continents, is that within those vast sedimentary layers, which are often stacked like pancakes with billions of creatures entombed therein (99% of which are marine creatures), are iron-rich minerals which oriented to the direction that the magnetic pole was at the time of the sedimentary deposition.

These magnetic reversals occurred while the sediments were accumulating to form the massive sedimentary layers which we see up on the continents, and these same reversals are reflected in lava rocks on the ocean-floor near the mid-oceanic rift zones which took only about two weeks to cool into hard rock,[4] so obviously, the magnetic reversals were occurring within a matter of days, and therefore, the sediments up on the continents were accumulated there within a matter of days, in fact, during about one year's time, as described, like an entry in a ship's log, by Noah about the Deluge in Genesis.

As also described in my first book, the lack of radial tension-cracks in the now-folded sedimentary rock-layers of the mountains shows that those sedimentary layers were still wet and soft when the folding occurred, during the mountain uplifts, that is, the mountains rose at the close of the Deluge (so the Flood water did not cover the current mountains), and so, the ancient primordial mound, symbolized with the Great Pyramid, is ruined somewhere under thousands of feet of Deluge sediments.

Most of the exposed lava rock of the earth are pillow basalts, which are dark iron-rich and silica-poor volcanic extrusions which look like stacks of pillows, and which look that way because they extruded-up into overlying water, that was during the Deluge when run-away plate tectonics were separating Pangea, and oceanic plates were diving rapidly under continental plates to heat at depth and rise as batholiths under Flood lain sediments, and continental plates cracked from extension forces which allowed basalt to flow up from the mantle of the earth into the Deluge water to become pillow basalts.

Mount Ararat in eastern Turkey is a mountain of pillow basalts that rose-up through the receding Flood waters (which slid off the continents into the then deepening ocean basins), but Genesis says that Noah's Ark landed in the Mountains of Ararat, so not necessarily on that biggest mountain in that mountainous pillow-basalt area, nonetheless, you can see that the mountains on which the remnant landed had just risen-up through the receding Deluge waters, and the other mountains of folded sedimentary layers (like the Himalayas) were rising-up because of regional compression, as continental crustal plates crashed into other continental plates (such as the India plate into the Asia plate, to form the Himalayas).

Early on, the progeny of Noah (also known as Manu, Noe, Oannes, Ziasudra, etc.) began to worship the sun god, rather than the God of Noah, and the sun god was to them symbolic of Adam, the first man, whom the Egyptians referred to as Atum-Re, the self-created form of the sun god, who was the first man in the Zep Tepi,[5] on the original primordial mound, which had emerged from the waters at creation. So this was an early form of ancestor worship, with the pharoahs' being the progeny of the sun god Atum (Adam) Re, as the then recently having had died Osiris pharoah resurrected as the next Horus pharaoh, like the sun returns from the underworld to resurrect at dawn. (From Re we get ray, as in sun ray.)

Two sons of Atum-Re (Adam) were the good Osiris and the evil Set, and Set killed his good brother, and that good brother, Osiris, resurrected as the new sun, Horus, Osiris' son (the next pharaoh), to overcome the evil deeds of Set. In the Biblical account, Seth (Set) is the Horus figure because he replaced his brother Abel who had been killed by the evil Cain, so it seems that the ancient Egyptians confused the story, made Cain (Osiris) to be the victim, instead of Abel, and the actual replacement for the murdered Abel, Seth, was made the bad guy (Set) who killed Osiris, and thereby, as they made Cain (Osiris) to be the good guy, they completely changed the lines of the good and the evil in pre-Deluge times.

Apparently, pre-Deluge clans had already bastardized the

story of Cain, Abel, and Seth to symbolize the battle of the sun's light, the supposed elixir of life, against darkness, the harbinger of death and hibernation, and they deliberately juxtaposed the players in the drama to make the good guy into the bad guy, and to make the new good guy, Osiris, who was actually Cain, to have the son Horus, who was actually the Seth character replacing the murdered Abel (he who was murdered actually by Cain), to tout this replacement "savior" Horus (actually Seth) as symbolic of all that is good, the symbol of the "resurrected" sun at dawn.

The Manu of the Rig Veda of ancient India was said to have been a child of the sun, and the Mountain of Manu, to the west of the Great Pyramid, was the land of the Set-ting sun, the land of death,[6] the land where the dead sun (where the dead pharaoh is protected by Osiris in the underworld) rejuvenates as the new pharaoh, symbolized by the ensuing new dawn sun, so the mass death that enveloped the world with the Deluge, which was survived by Thoth (the "heart of Re, which brings back the sun daily") and the Seven Sages,[7] is characterized with the symbol of death, in the case of the Mountain of Manu, and with the symbol of life after death, as the Hindu Manu was the progenitor of the new people who repopulated the earth after the pre-Kali yuga cataclysm of mass death, which was Noah's Flood, survived by Manu (Noah) and the Seven Rishis, who survived that Deluge which was noted by all the ancient civilizations and many tribal traditions.

According the ancient Babylonian tradition, the fish-humans Oannes and the Seven Apkallu survived the Deluge which was sandwiched between ten pre-Deluge kings and a line of post-Deluge kings noted by Berosus (which properly should be counted back to about 2200 B.C., as previously reasoned), and additionally, as Alexander the Great wrote that the Babylonians had been making precise astronomical measurements since 1903 years before the date of his writing at 331 B.C., so Babylon (Sumer) began in 2234 B.C.,[8] which lines-up nicely with the Global Flood Model (GFM).

The ancient Babylonians said that the reigns of the ten pre-Deluge kings lasted the precession number of 432,000 years (120 saris of 3,600 years each), so as we discussed, like the Hindu yugas of time which are multiples of 432,000 years, it is apparent that humans could not have been counting years that far back (even if the world was as the Darwinists say), and the likelihood that universal precession number, which is represented with the astronomically-derived dimensions of the Great Pyramid, would just happen to be the number of years until a worldwide cataclysm is obviously highly problematic, so since precession numbers symbolically dominate so many ancient legends, it is obvious that the number 432 is a manifestation of their ancient measurements of the precession of the earth's axis with the archaeometer. There can be no other reason.

Oannes was seen as a sort of sea monster, but a great educator and civilizer, who went below the sea at night (Set sun), and who rose the next morning to continue his good works, despite his seemingly monstrous reptilian nature,[9] a sort of fear and loathing, but with respect, sort of thing, like the pharoahs' wearing cobras on their head-garbs, and like the Nagas of India who were snake-worshippers, and who were reputed to have been the progeny of Asshur (also the father of the Azura Mazdas of Persia[10]), who was a son of Shem, and who was the founder of the earliest dynasty of Assyria (as Pusur-Asshur I).

This Asshur was the patron ancestor-god of the Assyrians for centuries, and so we see more veneration of created beings (ancestor worship) as if they were not corporal, like Adam was worshipped as Atum, a facet of the sun god, and as Noah was worshipped as the fish-man Oannes, the sun god, who set at night to return the next day to help mankind in his monstrous reptilian sort of way. The ancient Babylonians, who were closely integrated with the ancient Assyrians, worshipped the sun god Shamash, the namesake of Shem, who was the father of Asshur, so all in the family.

The Azuras who had moved south into India to become the snake-worshipping Naga-Dravidians (who "charm" snakes to this day) adopted Kasyapa as the sun god,[11] who was not a real person, but was the sun god who was the father of everything in creation, a god of solar pan-spermia. Another ancient sun god of India was Agni, who is mentioned with precession numbers in the Vedic legends, as previously noted, and who was said to breathe life into newborns when they open their mouths,[12] just as breath supposedly returns to the sun god when a person dies, when the Egyptians performed the ceremony of the opening of the mouth, as was true with the associated component of their solar religion where the soul dies with Osiris, but then resurrects with Horus (the namesake for the word hours).

This notion of the sun being the source of everything, including the breath of life, was rampant when Sundaland and the Pacific islands were being settled, as those ancient Lapita people also thought that the breath of life could be captured in statues, like the Egyptians thought that dead souls could manifest in statues, in amulets, hamulets, as it were, named after Noah's son Ham, the Khem who helped found Egypt, and whose namesake is also the term Chem in chemistry, and Cam in Gulf of Cambay (of northwestern India, where are some submerged Ice Age cities), the Cam in Cambodia, and with the Ham in Hampi of southern India. It is corroborative that the ancient Cam writing of Cambodia was a derivation of the ancient Sanskrit writing from India.

This spirit in the breath from the sun god could create magic on earth through the spirits' earthly homes, from the amulets and statues which were so revered by the ancients to have been affective spirit abodes. The huge stone heads of Easter Island, a few hundred miles west of South America, are representative of these earthly homes for spirits, for the earthly astral-doubles of the astral entities which are stars, or are of their supposed father, the sun. It is a sort of astral projection, with the ancestors affecting the happenings on earth by magic, through their amulet or statuary earthly-homes, the type of idolatry condemned in the Bible.

Is it not remarkable that God blew into molded clay (an amulet, so to speak) to make Adam come alive? This event of the six days of creation has obviously since been memorialized with this astral-projection notion that the sun and stars can inhabit animate and inanimate objects, a sort of limited pantheism which excludes the true Creator, this is quite a strange state of affairs, as the sun was mislabeled to be the creator of everything, which is of course an oxymoronic notion, because a created thing can't possibly be also the creator of itself.

This spirit-double of a being was known by the ancient Egyptians to be the person's ka, his astral double, who could also become a star, or a consort with Osiris and Horus and the father, Atum-Re, who actually was the first man Adam, and who is memorialized with the great Sphinx, the man-lion, who symbolized Atum-Re, and who faced the rising sun (Atum-Re) of the summer solstice before the Great Pyramid of Giza.

The Sphinx is the amulet for the ka of Atum, the self-created aspect of Re, who became the first being on the primordial mound at creation, so the Great Pyramid supposedly beckons immortality because it relates distance/time of the Wheel of Time through the dimensions of the Great Pyramid's being a microcosm of the dimensions of the earth. And by beckoning the spirit of the supposed aspect (Atum) of the creator god (Re), whose spirit as man and creator could influence the affairs of men through the amulet (the Sphinx) for his ka, the great Sphinx, facing due east from the base of the Great Pyramid, was the centerpiece of the ancient Egyptian religio-political state.

The ancient historian Constantinius Manasses said that dynastic ancient Egypt (when the Great Pyramid was built) began 1663 years before the date 526 B.C., when the Egyptian dynastic line was ended by the army of Cambyses of Persia, so the Great Pyramid and the Egyptian civilization of this post-Deluge era were begun in 2188 B.C., again fitting nicely within the chronology for the GFM (the Global Flood Model).

Kush, a son of Cham (Khem in Egypt), was quite the ranger like his father, and this son Kush founded the first dynasty in Mesopotamia at his namesake city of Kish, and the nation of Ethiopia was known as the Land of Kush, and the mountains to the northeast of the Indus-Sarasvati civilization are the Hindu-Kush, and a territory there is called Kash (Kush)-mere, so we see that this Kush, the father of Nimrod, and son of Cham, was a dominant figure early during the post-Deluge repopulation of the earth.

It is corroborative that God told Noah where in the world

his three sons' progenies would settle, with those of Shem settling essentially in western Asia, and those of Japheth settling in eastern and western Europe, and those of Cham allowed the exploration and settlement of the rest of the regions of the world. And so, as the seafaring Canaanites (Phoenicians), Khemites (Egyptians), and the Tamils (Naga-Dravidians) were the progenies of Cham (as well as of Asshur, a son of Shem, in the case of the Tamils of early India), we see that Cham's offspring had the mathematical and astronomical knowledge to achieve the great surveying and mapping projects that are evidenced with the precession-derived dimensions of the Great Pyramid, and with the maps of the ancient sea kings, showing that these children of Cham were aggressively settling in many parts of the globe, in search of riches and comfort, leaving behind for us to see their most ancient rock-hewn terraced plazas, pyramids, and temples, which defy the notion that they were built by unsophisticated proto-cavemen plunking along in crude canoes with a few rock and stick-tools to bump into lands over the distant horizons of the sea, with their fingers in the wind, and not much else of a clue.

And the ships which the children of Cham built to navigate the globe sometimes symbolized the celestial voyage which royalty would take in their afterlife, as we saw the buried seagoing ships near the Great Pyramid that were the ka's (the doubles) of the "solar boats" which carried the gods of the Egypt during their voyages across the sky and into the netherworld (like the sun sets), to return later in the solar boat of Horus, the risen sun.

The notion of boats for the afterlife was also prevalent among the Ice Age Europeans, who sent their heroes of into the sunset in their boats which had been set ablaze, like the sun setting into the netherworld at dusk. And many tribes of Asia have the same tradition to send the dead off in boats with torches to the netherworld, like the Egyptians believed that the god-men entered the bark of Re, or the bark of Horus, to sail around the spherical celestial ocean, as the sun and constellations move in their orderly paths along that "arch of the sky," and so, the "round face of the earth" could be measured with the archaeometer, as evidenced with the astronomically-derived dimensions of the Great Pyramid of Giza.

Spherical geometry is the basis of modern astronomy, because the stars do seem to move around a sphere as they follow their paths, to seem to rise and move across the arch of the sky to disappear again over the horizon, and then to continue on their paths "under the earth," to rise the next evening to complete the circuits around the sphere of the celestial ocean.

And the ancients thought that they could experience immortality as passengers in a solar boat, or in a stellar boat, that would ride on the spherical face of the "ocean" of the universe, which symbolized the cataclysmic global Deluge which covered the spherical face of the earth, on which the remnant eight survived in their "boat" which later was symbolized as the solar boat of life, the boat for one to escape eternal death, like the remnant eight used the earthly boat to survive the total destruction of the Deluge.

15
CHAPTER

Religion of Precession from the Ancients

Just as the ancient Phoenicians told curious potential high-seas navigators from competing nations that they might fall off of the edge of the globe, or be eaten by dreadful sea monsters, should they decide to navigate the high seas, so also, the priesthoods of the other sun-worshipping civilizations of the Ice Age went about their business of consolidating their political power by claiming mystical knowledge about the celestial realms which supposedly affected life on earth through the statues and amulets which played such a meaningful role in the lives of those ancients that those ancients thought the celestial powers could cause or prevent human events.[1]

And because celestial precession-measuring with the archaeometer by the Ice Age ancients for their precise mapping and surveying was the trade-secret of some of the rich and powerful in those days, who vigorously guarded their knowledge (in order to have the upper-hand in daily dealings), and because the precession measurement numbers are evident in the architectures, religious legends, stone-circles, and number systems of those ancients, it is evident that to hold a relative monopoly on their knowledge of the methodology to measure the movements of the constellations, which the ancients considered to be their starry celestial afterlife homes, would entail the control of building projects, and associated trade, and political decisions, because these elites better understood the supposed celestial homeland, which ostensibly affects life on earth through the animate and the inanimate, and therefore, they would dominate religious life, and so then, engender much sway with the people of those burgeoning Ice Age civilizations.

In ancient Egypt, during the few centuries of serious pyramid building which followed the Deluge, the Sages, the Apkallu, the Rishis, the great civilizers, carried forth for their progenies the lofty math/astronomy and associated engineering skills which manifested in that magnificent stone-block edifice of astronomically-derived dimensions, the Great Pyramid of Giza, there on the ancient Prime Meridian, from where the geographical distances and directions were triangulated according to the rate of precession, with the archaeometer, to be recorded as the maps of the ancient sea kings, which show startlingly accurate geographical locations, so accurate that such accuracy would not be matched until modern times.

Those ancient masters of "celestial mapping" carried such clout that they were seen as gods by subsequent generations, because they had come-over from the previous world when people lived much longer, in the pre-Deluge "Golden Age," the Zep Tepi of the Egyptians, when the Akhus (human-lions, like Atum) lived great numbers of years, but then all went sour, and the "gods" became angry with humanity, and so, brought the Deluge to purge the evil from the earth, And the dead, like Osiris, the symbolic king of the Zep Tepi, rose victorious as his own son Horus, the sun of the dawn, who rises to rejuvenate in the new post-Deluge world, which, according to the ancients, happened because the World Tree was shaken when the sun, circa 2400 B.C., moved into its new Aries house, and so then, the World Tree, atop which resides the Dragon, was shaken to cause the Deluge.

After being retrieved from his wooden coffin which supposedly floated on the water to become a part of the symbolic World Tree of the Temple of Baalbeck in Canaan, Osiris was said to have been buried at Sokar, which is the Giza Plateau,[2] where are the Sphinx and Great Pyramid. And in being buried in the earth, the dead symbolic king Osiris from the pre-Deluge world was thereby entombed in the earth like the victims of the Deluge had been entombed in the earth, within the sedimentary layers caused by the global flood.

But this Osiris lived-on through his son Horus, the morning sun,[3] because he knew the celestial way to immortality, based upon the knowledge of the imagined drama of the stars as they appear to move along the horizon, causing the sun to come alive in new houses every 2,160 years, because of the slow wobble of the earth's axis, at the top of which is Draco, the Dragon, who can be imagined to be the engine of this precession of the constellations.

In the night sky over Egypt circa 2200 B.C., when the Great Pyramid and Sphinx were being built, the constellation of Orion "the Hunter" was thought by the Egyptians to have been the ka (spirit-double) of Osiris, the king from the First Time, from the Zep Tepi, who was then betrayed by his cosmic brother Set and the 72 conspirators (the rate of precession) at the time of the shaking of the World Tree (the Djed in Egypt) which supposedly caused the Deluge.

The constellation Orion (Osiris) seemed to stand-up during its passage along the arch of the sky, and at the summer solstice when the Nile peaks, those ancient Egyptians saw that Orion seemed to rise from the horizon just before the sun peeked-up at dawn, so they equated the resurrected Orion (Osiris) with the rising longest summer sun, the resurrected new pharoah, sun Horus, which in those centuries on the summer solstice was rising in front of the star Regulus,[4] the heart of the constellation Leo, the lion, the man-lion who was Atum (actually Adam), who with his offspring were symbolized as lions (the Akhu, the Shining Ones, who recited formulae like precession maths, they were the Sages, some of whom survived the Deluge)[5], as with the lion-figure of the Sphinx, which was said to have been the living image of Atum, that is, the Sphinx was the statue (hamulet, or amulet) in which abided the astral spirit, the ka of Atum, who was the first man, the first Shining One, the first Sage, and self-created aspect of the sun god Re.

So humans were seen as manifestations of the sun and stars, as astral extensions to create humans (children of the sun), and animals, and even inanimate things, like the Sphinx, which was said to have been the living image of Atum, and like the three Pyramids of Giza (one of which is the Great Pyramid), which are aligned like Orion's Belt of the constellation of Orion (Osiris), the pre-Deluge king who "resurrected."[6]

The new pharaoh was the enlightened new son (Horus) of the sun, who was ushered in with Osiris' annual resurrection, just before dawn on the summer solstice every year, when the sun was beginning to leave its house in Taurus for Aries, on the horizon straight to the east from Giza, at the rate of 72 years/degree, the transition which just previously had supposedly caused the Deluge, which evidently occurred barely this side of 2400 B.C. So one more zodiac age from about 2350 B.C. (forward 2,160 years through Aries) was at about 200 B.C., when a shaking of the World Tree was then expected by many,[7] but never happened when the sun entered its then new house of Pisces. Obviously, the ancients quickly learned that a cataclysm does not occur with every change of the sun's house every 2,160 years, which many religio-precession sages of astronomy and astrology were at that time predicting.

The change from one age of the zodiac to next, because of precession, had only been previously witnessed by the eight fish-humans who survived the Deluge, when the sun moved from its house in Taurus (the Bull) into its then new house in Aries (the Ram) at around 2350 B.C., so since the World Tree folks thought that the Tree was shaken when the sun moved into its new house every 2,160 years, predictions of calamity ran rampant wherever earth-hexagon math and astronomy and their bi-produced astrological religions were flourishing, which was throughout the Middle East, in Central America, South America, east Asia, and India.

But no global cataclysm has happened since the Deluge, as the sun has now entered its third house since then, now in the constellation of Aquarius, having just vacated Pisces. But students of Mayan precession religion say that the year 2012 A.D., according to their take on the state of the sun's transition into Aquarius, will be the time to expect a new sun, so to speak, after another global cataclysm, the exact nature of which is unclear, and so, I suppose "unknown."

Although there has been only one global cataclysm which men have recorded, the Deluge, it is a bit odd that people throughout the ages have looked to a time after 2,160 more years when the house of the sun would again change, and so, another global cataclysm would supposedly ensue because the World Tree of ancient religions would then again be shaken. But we have had just one global cataclysm within the three sun house-changes since about 2400 B.C., so what's the point with these precession-related chronologies of many ancient traditions?

There are no accounts of a global catastrophe from 2,160 years before the Deluge, that would have been at circa 4500 B.C., when Hancock and Schoch would have us believe that the ancients were measuring precession and building advanced megaliths, and so, would have noted that supposed change of the sun's house, but there are no records of a sun house-change then, nor of any global cataclysm which precession religionists would have expected then, so here we now have four sun house-changes which might have caused global cataclysms. But does this so-called World Tree really do any shaking at the expected times? Apparently not so.

The only documented global cataclysm in human history is the Deluge, which did happen to have occurred at the time of a sun house-change, but the other house-changes came with no pop, no fizz, and therefore, religio-sciences based upon precession arithmetic are plainly specious, and are nothing more than vain attempts to derive eternal meanings from the movements of created things, because from stars and their movements, we are supposed to determine things eternal. This is the ultimate merger of science with religion to attempt to explain purpose through science, in other words, it's an absurd attempt to quantify the eternal.

With the Babylonians figuring 432,000 years (120 saris of 3,600 years each) before the Deluge back to the creation, and the ancient Hindus counting multiples of 432,000 years in between global cataclysms (of which there is evidence of actually only one, the Deluge), and with Herodotus saying that some Egyptians said that their civilization went back the precession number of 10,800 years, and other Egyptians saying that the Bennu bird (the Phoenix) returns after half of a precession cycle, after 12,954 years, to start a new post-cataclysmic world,[8] and since the only cataclysm mentioned in Egyptian history is the Deluge, it is evident that these groups were measuring chronologies by celestial math, and not by true years.

And the Mayans counted back precessionally the "suns," which supposedly have been global cataclysms at multiple episodes of sun house changes through millions of precession-number-counted years, nonetheless, we see that only one global cataclysm has actually occurred which vividly lingered in the collective-mind of the ancients, the Deluge.

But the other cataclysms claimed to have occurred (of which there is no geological evidence) go back impossibly long, and clearly precession-number-based, amounts of time, therefore are lacking evidences of buildings, or signs of developing culture, or historical records, from the supposed 8,000 years (or 432,000 years) between when the great megalithic structures were built circa 2000 B.C., and when these precession-counters would have been counting the precession-denominated numbers of years mentioned above, and so presumably leave signs of their precession-counting culture, certainly from by circa 10000 B.C., if not all the way back 432,000 years, to when "early cavemen" would have supposedly begun that big precession count of years (with their fingers, and toes?).

The Bennu (Bennyx, the Phoenix) Bird of Egypt was said to have landed on the phallus of Osiris to rejuvenate him, to rebirth him, as his son Horus, the new dawn sun, who rises in a new house every 2,160 years, and so, is the one constant through the Wheel of Time, when the house for the sun changes, but the occupant of the merry-go-round of changing houses, the sun, does not, as does not that entity atop the celestial pole, the Dragon, who seems to be the engine of the Wheel of Time, as the constellations seem to rotate around his high place which does not move from the celestial axis of the earth.

The Bennu bird was also thought to immolate himself upon a pyre of fire (symbolizing the sun) when he returned, and then would reincarnate as the resurrected Bennu bird for the then post-cataclysmic new age, and would fly back into the heavens, to return again later after presumably six more sun house-changes, to usher in another post-cataclysmic new age, which according to some ancient Egyptian buffs was almost 13,000 years ago (half a precession cycle ago, 12,960 years), and so, like the Mayan religionists, they are now expecting another global cataclysm, as it is again time for the supposed return of the Phoenix (Bennu bird), to usher in a new age, and to reincarnate and fly back to the heavens as a sign that life continues after global cataclysms.

Because the Ice Age is commonly thought to have ended about that 13,000 number of years ago (which is "coincidently" about half of a precession cycle ago), it is presumed by Hancock and his ilk that the widespread ancient legends about the global Deluge were actually describing the sea level rise at the end of the Ice Age when about 25 million square miles of lowlands succumbed to the sea. But we have seen that this notion is as absurd as it is convenient for the likes of Hancock and Schoch because they can say that the Deluge did occur at the precession time of half a precession cycle ago (when pop science says that the Ice Age melted and sea level rose a few hundred feet), but they, in so doing, must ignore the plain language of hundreds of ancient legends that the Deluge was a global cataclysm.

And they must claim to see what is not actually in the geological record, and they must explain why other precession religionists, contradictorily, say that the cataclysms caused by the shaking of the World Tree are global, and not merely localized calamities of water or fire (and the over 500 ancestral legends about global cataclysm are all about the Deluge), yet Hancock and Schoch blatantly bastardize these traditions such that the Deluge which covered the earth was "really" just a sea level rise engulfing a bit of the edges of the continental landmasses, to fit with what popular science says about the timing of the end of the Ice Age.

This unconscionable distortion of the facts in their attempts to fit pop science with precession religion, astrological faith, and new age karma, is intriguing to observe evolve, as the only way out for the naysayers of the Genesis account is to go their route of blatant and tortuous distortions of the evidences. The ancient accounts are clear that the worldwide Deluge occurred within human history, at the time of a house-change for the sun, which was circa 2350 B.C., when the sun was moving from Taurus (the Bull) into Aries (the Ram), statues and gods of which were legion in the ancient world, along the with the dragon of Draco, the lions of the sun god (and his progeny), and the serpent/dragon of Draco, which was associated with the sun god, such as the sun god Quetzacoatl of the Mayans, who was depicted in a rock sculpture as the sun with a serpent-head coming forth from its center.[9]

At the (pre-Mayan) Olmec stepped Pyramid of Kukulcan (another name of Quetzacoatl) in southern Mexico, the shadow of the serpent, symbolizing the sun god, undulates up the steps of that great pyramid of sun worship as progresses the morning of the spring equinox, the time when life is thought to regenerate. This serpent of the sun is also depicted in ancient art sculpture as a plumed serpent, and in fact, Quetzacoatl and Kukulcan both mean plumed or feathered serpent.

Sounds like the feathers of the Bennu (Bennyx) bird of Egypt, the Phoenix, who when working with the movements of the sun into its new house would allegedly come to earth to die and rise again at the time of a global cataclysm, to fly up again into the heavens, where is the sun, and where is the serpent Draco, who seems to lord over the whole precession process from his unchanging position high above the earth's axis at the apex of the celestial sphere which encompasses the sphere of the earth.

The Egyptian Horus king, the risen sun, the new pharaoh, was symbolized as a hawk in the ancient hieroglyphic writings, and the pharoah wore a snake amulet over his forehead, and the hood of the cobra, the uraeus, on his head as a sign of celestial wisdom, cunning, and virtual omnipotence, so here we see another link that the serpent at the top of the Djed, the World Tree of the Egyptians, was perhaps a flying serpent, who was symbolized by both the Bennu bird of precession, and the hawk of Horus, the sun god, who was often associated with the serpent in the ancient world, like the self-proclaimed children of the sun of ancient India, the Nagas of Asshur (who was a son of Shem), who worshipped the serpent, and who obviously saw the serpent of the sun as their father.

And because they were precession-savvy with their stone-circles and their precession-number-embodied megalithic ceremonial buildings, like at Arunachela in southern India, which is the base 6 number 48 degrees east of Giza, and as the sun temple at Angkor Wat in Cambodia is 72 degrees east of Giza, and Sao Pa of the ancient Jomon on Taiwan is 90 degrees east of Giza, and Pachamac in Peru is 144 degrees east of Giza, they also saw this serpent as being of Draco, at the top of the universe, there unchanging, and working with the predictably-moving sun, so that mankind can survive the supposed shaking-of-the-World-Tree-caused global cataclysms, the Deluge being allegedly but one of a series of these, which supposedly occurred after impossibly too long to have actually been counted numbers of years, so plainly, here we are dealing with merely calculated precession-denominated epochs of time which were schemed by the ancient precession religionists, who reverenced the Dragon atop the World Tree, and who imagined that he controls the supposed predictably periodic cataclysms.

Much of the world was gripped with this precession religion deriving from the guarded knowledge by the ancient elites about the precession of the earth's axis, and about how the rate of precession was utilized to measure and map the earth, so now, we still see a preoccupation with such in the world today, as people seek-out the meaning of life by measuring the movements of the stars and planets, through astrology, seeking meaning in the movements of created entities, rather than seeking meaning in the Creator of those things.

The religions based upon the movements of the sun, planets, and stars continue to have huge followings today, predicated upon this ancient precession knowledge which enabled the ancients to effectively chart the surface sphere of the earth by charting the movements of the sun and stars along the apparent celestial sphere of the universe. So in quoting the occultists, "as it is above, so it is here below," we see that the celestial bodies are supposedly somehow alive and have influence on the affairs of humankind, and thereby, unfortunately, we today have a woefully serious and deep-seeded spiritual pandemic, with humans worshipping the creation, rather than the Creator, and this is the ultimate spiritual deception.

Epilogue

As I continue to read more about the submerged megaliths in various parts of the world, the profusion of them is almost mind-boggling. Submerged megalithic ruins are said (by the local fishermen) to extend intermittently from near Mahabalipuram, off the southeast coast of India, down along that coast about two hundred miles to the southern tip of India, these are all of the ancient kingdom of Kumari Kandam, but who will explore, map, and film them? Will it be you?

And Ibrahim Darwish of the Department of Antiquities of Egypt says that there are about 35 submerged sites extending west from Alexandria, from the submerged ruins of Herakleion, west to Sollom, which is about a hundred-twenty miles of submerged megalithic sites, so obviously, there is much more investigating to be done, but who will do it?

We must pressure archaeologically-minded institutions to spend some money to explore this virtually untapped submerged world of archaeological interest, it is a travesty that more has not been done to this point in time, but the "submergies" are down there, just waiting to be fully documented by camera, and then to be explained vis-à-vis the timing of the end of the Ice Age, the end of it which must have been much later than is popularly declared by conventional scientists.

The website of the Hellenic (Greek) Ministry of Culture says that there are submerged megalithic ruins off Plytra, Platygiali, Astakos, and Abdera, and ruins are said to be off Epidauros there near Athens, so a rich field of subjects awaits the underwater photographer in the Greek isles, so let's go. And the submerged city off Elafonisi Island, about sixty miles northwest of Crete, is just begging to be photographed more fully.

The submerged ruins off Elafonisi are twenty-one acres of tightly constructed hewn megalithic building remains, complete with grids of streets, just like the Mycenaen constructions still onshore, which do resemble the ancient constructions in the Andes, in the South Pacific, in North Africa, and in southern Spain, the ruins of the ancient city-states of the Ice Age precession navigators, who were navigating the globe during the Ice Age, laying hold of mineral-rich lands and then building these megalithic structures.

The many submergie sites off southern Spain of "Atlantis" (off Chipiona, Rota, Huelva, and Tarifa) look like those still onshore at Niebla, so they were obviously built around the same time, around 2000 B.C., and then the Ice Age ended to submerge "Atlantis," a name after Atlas (the namesake of the nearby Atlas Mountains of Morocco), who is said to have been a son of Sidon, also known as the ancestor god Poseidon (Father Sidon), and who apparently joined forces with the advanced navigators of his original homeland of the patriarch Canaan (who was a son of Ham, and Sidon's father) to navigate, map, and settle in much of the world.

Plato wrote that Solon of Egypt at around 600 B.C. said that Atlantis went under 9,000 years before that time, but he also said that Athenian kings of Greece (of circa 1500 B.C.), Erechtheus, Cecrops, and Erichthonius, were fighting against the Atlanteans in the Mediterranean at the time that Atlantis (and the Greek sites mentioned above, and the rest of the submergies worldwide) went under, so obviously, a zero was added to 900 years for the date of the submergence of Atlantis. It is certainly odd that Plato, a Greek, did not notice this discrepancy, however, the Greeks were in awe of the Egyptians, and seemed to hang-on their every word, so it seems that Plato brushed this discrepancy under the rug.

The extensive submergie ruins off Lebanon (Canaan) also beg to be fully photographed, these submerged ruins of ancient Sidon (son of Canaan) and Yarmuta, off the coast of Lebanon, have rarely been seen, so I ask that somebody get over there and film them for the world to see, it's too important to not be common knowledge, so let's do it.

Submergie megalithic ruins of the ancient kingdom of Ys are said to be on the shallow seafloor of the Bay of Dourarnenez, off the western coast of France, near the beach of Le Ris, near the coast town of Brest, and the ruins of a submerged city-state are reputed to be on the bottom of Britain's Cardigan Bay, off the coast of Wales (the submerged ruins of Cantre'r Gwaelod), as well as, off the Isles of Scilly, and off Cornwall in Britain (the submerged ruins of Lyonesse), so let's get rolling.

The world needs to know about the many ruins on the shallow seafloor which were submerged when the Ice Age ended for sea level to rise and cover about 25 million square miles of land worldwide, when the great Indus, Egyptian, and Sumerian civilizations went into decline, as those regions turned to dust with the end of the Ice Age, when the great migrations of people groups, such as of the "Sea Peoples," began in response to the then drastically changing climate, and to the sea level rise which consumed so much of their settled land.

The ancient Greco-Roman geographer Strabo wrote (in his *Geography* 7-2.1) that the Celts of southern Britain said that much land off the Cornwall coast succumbed to the sea long ago, and the ancient Roman historian Diodorus Siculus wrote (in his *Biblioteca Historica*, book 5, chapter 47, 4) about a legend from Samothrace, which is an island in the northern Aegean, off the northwest coast of Turkey, about 50 miles southeast from Abdera of northeast Greece:

> *The inhabitants who were caught in the flood ran up to higher regions of the island. And when the sea kept rising higher and higher, they prayed to the native gods, and since their lives were spared, to commemorate their rescue, they set up boundary stones around the entire circuit of the island, and dedicated altars upon which they offer sacrifices even to the present day."*

From the preceding passage from Diodorus Siculus, we can

see that the ancients of Samothrace experienced a limited sea level rise, the limited sea level rise caused by the end of the Ice Age, and obviously, not the global encompassing catastrophe which was the Deluge of Noah (who was known as Deucalion to the Greeks), which occurred about eight hundred years before this limited sea level rise described by the ancient inhabitants of Samothrace, there in the northern Aegean.

On the shallow seafloor in the North Sea, some 60 miles northwest of the German city of Bremerhaven, and about 5 miles east of the island of Helgoland, are the legendary submerged ruins of Basileia. The ruins of the megalithic palace of this Ice Age city-state have been noted by divers, but someone should dive there to photograph those ruins which undoubtedly will look similar to the polygonal megalithic block walls and citadels of the submergies off southern Spain and Greece, and to those off the northern coast of Egypt.

We have seen that the dimensions of Egypt's Great Pyramid at Giza are a reduced embodiment of the dimensions of the earth, and so, our nautical-mile system is from the same mold as the ancient system which assigned the base-perimeter length of the Great Pyramid to be the equivalent of half a nautical mile (1,760 royal cubits of 20.632 inches each), therefore, both systems relate time to distance, in the case of the ancient system, by the rate of precession (with the archaeometer), and in the case of the modern system, by measuring the rate of the apparent movement of the sun during a 24 hour period (with Harrison's Chronometer), both predicated on the earth hexagon to establish the radius length of the earth, so the systems are essentially one and the same, both measuring celestial body movements vis-à-vis their positions relative to positions on the earth, "measuring the round face of the earth on the arch of the sky," as the ancient Olmecs used to say.

Ever wonder why there are 1,760 yards per statute mile? It is because the ancestral knowledge of the subdivision of the base-perimeter length of the Great Pyramid is the root of this, arbitrary at first glance, subdivision of the statute mile into 1,760 yards. There were 1,760 royal cubits to the base of the Great Pyramid, and there are 1,760 yards per statute mile, so this number is obviously a remnant of the ancient recollection from the times of the ancient sea kings during the Ice Age, when the Great Pyramid was built, and when the ancients were navigating and settling the globe, including England (from where our statute mile system originates).

And before the recent advent of the metric system in the Olympics, the athletes ran the 440 and 880 yard runs, obviously based upon the number of cubits of one base side and of two base sides of the Great Pyramid. The precession rate-derived royal cubit length standard (20.632 inches) was mostly lost through the millennia after the Ice Age, with new length standards, not based on precession, coming into vogue, but these ancient subdivision numbers are plainly grounded in the surveying technique for the Great Pyramid, so point this out to the naysayers, it is more hard evidence for the connection between the ancient precession system and our modern system of earth measuring.

Remember too that 12 inches to the foot, and 36 inches to the yard, are base 6 denominated, not base 5 or 10 denominated, as we would expect if the ancient number systems evolved when "cavemen" supposedly began to count their fingers and toes, which is what the Darwinists would predict, according to their dogma. Base 6 was the foundation of the ancient number systems, so it is no coincidence that the base 6 number of 24 hours per day was universally accepted as the number of hours (Horus) of the day, and not 20 hours or 25 hours as the Darwinists would predict because of cavemen's finger and toe counts for the basis of their numbering systems.

I strongly urge you to read *Maps of the Ancient Sea Kings* by Charles Hapgood, he duly concludes that those maps were from ancient source maps drawn during the Ice Age, with confirming opinions from cartography experts from the U.S. Air Force and from M.I.T., who agreed that the ancients were evidently navigating and mapping the globe during the Ice Age with incredible precision.

Point-out this material to your skeptical associates, it is a real eye-opener, and will engender much more healthy debate regarding when did the Ice Age actually end, and regarding how did the ancients effectively sail to and settle far-flung regions of the globe (when considered with the precession/hexagon mapping scheme presented in this book, *Ice Age Civilizations*, and in the DVD of the same name).

The ancient precession/hexagon mapping scheme has unfortunately been co-opted to deceive millions of people today through the "science" of astrology, which uses this scheme of the ancient mapping methodology, but espouses power from the stars and their movements to affect life on earth, when in reality, the courses of the stars were designed by the Creator such that ancient clans could measure and map the earth, by measuring the rate of precession, and by applying such to simple hexagon geometry, to be enabled to measure and map the earth.

This is a wonderful testament to the obvious created design of the universe, and this design was not intended to be worshipped through astrology, because astrology is the worship of the creation, rather than the Creator. The design of the universe was for admiring, and measuring, and not for worshipping. Please understand that God explicitly condemns astrology in the Bible, and states that the worship of the creation, rather than the Creator, is futile and destructive.

Thank you for coming along on this ride, and I trust that your eyes have been opened regarding the capabilities of the ancients, and the plausibility of the Genesis account. All of the Bible is demonstrably true, even Genesis, so I hope that you now use your God-given faith to accept the Son of God, one of the triune entities of the Godhead, Jesus Christ, who came to earth to physically die, and then rose from the dead, so that we can Spiritually live with Him forever. Amen.

Appendices

Appendix I

Article 11

from http://www.genesisveracity.com

Great Pyramid and the Astronomical Merry-Go-Round

Mainstream science received a hot potato as I have determined the methodology for the math which prescribed the dimensions of the Great Pyramid of Giza. Please enjoy, and note that it relates to the 72 conspirators against Osiris, to the 72 virgins of Islam, to the Hindu yugas of time that are multiples of 432,000 years, to the 432,000 warriors of Valhalla, to the 432,000 years of pre-Flood Babylonian kings' reigns, to the 360 year Babylonian period of time called the sari, to the 360 pre-Islamic Arab gods, to our 360 degree mapping system, to our base 60 timekeeping system, and to astrology. I hope that you send this message far and wide, as it reveals the ancient mapping and navigation underpinnings for the numerology of much of the occult world.

Thanks, **James I. Nienhuis**

The ancient Sumerians (Babylon) used a Base Six number system because they knew that the length of one side of a six-sided polygon (that is a hexagon) is the same length as is the radius of the circle that circumscribes this hexagon.

They also knew that the constellations of the zodiac seem to rotate along the horizon like a merry-go-round at a rate of 72 years per degree (per one degree of 360 degrees) of rotation which is known as the precession of the stars. This precession results from the slow wobble of the earth's axis (like a gyroscope) which would wobble once through one full 360 degree precession in 25,920 years (as 72 years x 360 degrees equals 25,920 years/360 degrees of precession).

The determination that the constellations of the zodiac "move" along the horizon at the rate of 72 years/degree was achieved through the utilization of the Celtic Cross, which was a 360 degree-scaled circular hub that was affixed to a cross which was orientated by a plumb-bob. A facsimile of this device was discovered within the Great Pyramid of Giza, and modern versions of it have proven to be superb navigational devices (see www.CrichtonMiller.com).

Because the radius-length of a circle is the same length as is the length of one side of the hexagon that is circumscribed by this circle, the determination of the length of one side of a hexagon that is circumscribed by the circle of the earth thereby determines the radius-length of the earth. As the precession of the zodiac would complete in 25,920 years, the ancients knew that 1/6th of 25,920 years (that is 4,320 years) would represent the "movement" of the zodiac along the length of one side of the earth hexagon.

The length of one side of the earth hexagon is therefore the distance traveled by the constellations of the zodiac along the horizon during 4,320 years, and through the use of the Celtic Cross, the ancients determined the locations on the earth's surface of the beginning and end of this side of the earth hexagon, they then subdivided this distance by 7,200 (based upon Base Six, and upon their desire for a practical unit of distance), which produced the "royal mile" that is about half the length of our current mile, and that was subdivided into 1,760 "royal cubits" which are 20.632 inches each.

Each side of the base of the Great Pyramid of Giza was designated 440 units of length (times 4 equals 1,760 units) because the whole number fraction of pi (22/7) when multiplied by 40/40 gives unit lengths for 2 sides and for the height of the Pyramid (880 royal cubits and 280 royal cubits), and thereby, convenient whole numbers were established with which to efficiently construct the Pyramid.

Since the 7,200 units of distance (which are royal miles) of one side of the earth hexagon, after being multiplied by six (as there are six sides of a hexagon) results in the figure 43,200, which just happens to be the factor that the earth's circumference is to the one royal mile perimeter-length (1,760 cubits) of the Great Pyramid of Giza, and that the earth's radius-length is to the height (280 royal cubits) of the Great Pyramid, it is obvious that the ancients could "measure the arch of the sky and the round face of the earth."

In fact, the ancients accurately mapped most of the world around 2000 B.C., and the evidences of their astro-navigational capabilities are found with the stone-circles and astronomically-aligned pyramids (both on land and sea-floor) that are located at strategic Base-Six-denominated longitudinal locations around the world, which established these megalithic sites as geographical reference points for the astronomical measurements and resultant mapping by the ancient seafarers.

Note: If the ancient Egyptians had subdivided the radius of the earth (and also therefore, one side of the earth hexagon) by 3,600 rather than 7,200, the royal mile would have been identical to the nautical mile, so it is obvious that our mapping and time-keeping systems are based upon the ancients' measurements of the earth's precession.

James I. Nienhuis http://www.GenesisVeracity.com

I hope that you contact me for interview (ph# 713-784-6618), and I encourage you to read Article #10 at the website as it puts this finding into historical context. Scientists are treating this finding as if it's kryptonite, what do you and your associates think about it? Do you see any flaws in the analysis?

Appendix II

http://www.prnewswire.co.uk/cgi/news/release?id=112524

Is the Celtic Cross Really the Key to the Door of Ancient Knowledge?

LONDON, England, November 20 /PRNewswire/ —ATTN Feature Editors

With picture A historical researcher dropped a controversial bombshell publicly for the first time at the Questing Conference in London on Saturday 15th December turning history and religion on its head.

The Questing Conference is an annual event organized for scientists and researchers from America and the United Kingdom whose interests lie in revisionist Archaeology and History.

Crichton E M Miller demonstrated an ancient device before a shocked audience. They were shocked because they had all seen the Celtic cross before, but had dismissed it as a religious icon rather than a scientific instrument.

The working Celtic cross explains the construction of pyramids and henges supporting the possibility of transatlantic voyages by mariners from Europe to America long before Christopher Columbus.

His live demonstration backed up with extensive research, proved beyond doubt that our prehistoric ancestors were capable of detailed surveying, astronomy, navigation, sophisticated mathematics and time keeping using the Celtic cross, which he has named an Archaeometer.

"The knowledge and wisdom were locked in stone for us to discover" he said to one reporter. "This cross is not to be confused with the Christian crucifix.

The older Pagan Celtic cross was probably absorbed in to the Christian Church along with many other ideas from pre history; we owe the church a debt of gratitude for preserving it for our children".

"It seems that many scientific and religious minds are locked in stone too or we would have known of it earlier"
When asked how he discovered it, he replied" Providence, diligence and an open mind" He went on to say

"The Celtic cross is an inspiring inheritance for everyone living in a free world, folk should have the opportunity to discover the truth about their intelligent ancestors for themselves."

When asked how and when he made the discovery, he answered "The eureka moment happened one November night in 1997. Most researchers have concentrated on how the Great Pyramid of Khufu (Cheops) was built and the stones were moved, no one asks how it was designed.

Everything starts somewhere and I wanted to go to the beginning, how was the pyramid measured.

All buildings need the skills of a surveyor before the architect can design the construction; The Great Pyramid is the largest and most accurately designed single building in the world even by today's standards, I put together a surveying instrument from the simple materials that were available to the Egyptians, I came up with a hand held instrument that is capable of full spherical geometry and accurate to 3 arc minutes, which according to Cambridge University is the amount that the pyramid is out by in its stellar alignments.

I went on to discover that parts of this instrument were still in a sealed chamber in the pyramid and that other parts had been removed in 1872 and now rest in the British Museum.

I have reassembled them and they work.

You see, it is the principle that counts, for the next six years my research revealed the Celtic cross for navigation, the stellar clock that they used and the ability to find longitude without a mechanical clock.

It is the root of our mathematics and our religions"

Crichton E M Miller was awarded two British Patents on this ancient forgotten design in 2000 and again in 2001.

He has had articles on archaeology printed in Ancient American, the Italian Hera Magazine and Practical Boatowner.

His work is already referenced by other researchers into ancient history.

A member of The Society of Authors and a qualified navigator, Crichton's book is one of the most profound enlightenments to come to light since the science of investigative archaeology began.

The *Golden Thread of Time* ISBN 0-9541639-0-7 is available by mail order through www.pendulumpublishing.com or www.amazon.co.uk at US$29.99 plus shipping

Average Amazon Customer Rating: *The Golden Thread of Time* ISBN 0-9541639-0-7
Customers gave *The Golden Thread of Time* an average rating of 5/5
Source: British Book Reviews
http://books.reviewindex.co.uk/reviews_uk/0954163907.html

A high resolution photograph accompanying this release is available to the media free of charge at www.newscast.co.uk (+44 207 608 1000)

Distributed by PR Newswire on behalf of Pendulum Publishing

Appendix III

http://heritage.scotsman.com/myths.cfm?id=2401602005

Henges, pyramids and the Celtic cross helped ancient mariners sail the world

by Diane MacLean

from the *Daily Scotsman* online newspaper

TIME is the most important commodity on earth. It gives order to our lives, determining whether we get to where we are meant to be and measuring out our allotted lifespan. We think we understand time and have mastered its intricacies. But how did we tell time centuries ago?

Our Neolithic ancestors looked to the sky for answers about time. Their skills were learnt from the position of the sun and moon and changes in nature. This basic time-keeping would not have given them a deep understanding of time and their place in the Universe.

But what if this picture were false? What if our distant ancestors were far from being the passive creatures upon whom time acted to their eternal ignorance? What if they had mastered time and that it was through one of the strongest icons of our past, the Celtic cross?

In his book The Golden Thread of Time, Crichton EM Miller looks at the possibility that what we recognise as a Celtic cross is an ancient navigational instrument.

Just such a proposal has been put forward by amateur historian, archaeologist and navigator Crichton EM Miller in his book The Golden Thread of Time that says he has found a tool that re-writes history:

"This magical instrument that I have discovered, hoary with age ... encompasses a knowledge of the cosmos, the use and understanding of mathematics, geometry, surveying, astronomy and astrology. The secrets of this device were foundations of ancient civilisations, long before the written world."

Miller says that with this instrument he can prove that the ancients could understand time, that they could plot where they were in position to stars, and most importantly in terms of travel, used this same instrument to find longitude.

Finding longitude - the ability to determine a point east or west of a chosen north-south line, or meridian - has been sailing's greatest quest. The British navy lost so many ships because of their inability to find their position accurately, that by the 18th century the race was on to discover an instrument to help. In the 1730s when John Harrison invented his chronometer and cracked the problem of longitude, navigation was changed forever.

Most archaeologists suggest that before being able to plot longitude, intercontinental ocean travel was impossible, or if achieved, relied on luck. They point out that longitude relies on knowing local time, and where, they ask, are the ancients' clocks?

Could the stone circle at Callanish on the Isle of Lewis be the remains of an ancient clock? Miller's answer is that they are right under our noses – in the henges and pyramids that exist throughout the world.

"I have discovered that these pyramids and megaliths are the clocks and calendars of the ancients," he says.

Miller believes that henges were used in the Northern Hemisphere (where the pole star is higher in the sky) and pyramids in the Southern Hemisphere as "star clocks or observatories". He concludes that these sophisticated structures were designed with the aid of an instrument that we recognise from graveyards and churches, but in its original form allowed an ancient understanding of the universe and time.

"The instrument of knowledge and practical skill is the cross," reveals Miller. "The Celtic cross is a practical working tool of great depth. It was the staff of magicians."

Miller came to his understanding of the practical purpose of the

Celtic cross whilst out at sea experimenting with finding the position of stars. He discovered that a simple protractor on a cross with a plumbline could define degrees. Since then, his experiments have concluded that this device can perform the minute geometric calculations necessary to build the pyramids, henges and ultimately enable timekeeping.

His theory is supported in part by a discovery in the Great Pyramid at Giza. In 1872 Waynman Dixon discovered a shaft in the Egyptian pyramid and hidden within found a number of broken objects, what look like a measuring stick, a plumbline and a hook. Miller suggests that this is part of the cross instrument used by Egyptians to measure and track the angle of stars. He postulates that the pyramid was the giant clock the Egyptians used to tell the time and that in this way Giza became the prime meridian against which local time was set throughout the rest of the world using megalithic henges or pyramids.

An ancient Mayan bowl quite clearly showing a celtic cross.
Miller also thinks that the knowledge of the cross came to Egypt from elsewhere, as evidenced by the stone henges in Britain which pre-date the pyramid at Giza. Miller believes Neolithic sailors navigated the seas with ease using their Celtic cross.

"A lot of the proof is similarity of design separated by ocean and time," he explains. "There are so many similarities in boats, language. Anomalies which cause problems to histories are solved by the early ability to navigate."

Miller has found numerous examples of cave drawings, rock art or decorative ceramics that include the Celtic cross. He has visited 26,000-year-old cave drawings that show the angle of the stars, "proving" the ancients' accurate knowledge of the solar system.

And with his discovery of an alternative history that demonstrates we were once all "children of the earth", Miller hopes to change the world.

"Today we're separated by concepts of nation," he says. "We have come through one of the worst centuries ever – millions slaughtered on ideas. Perhaps if we could accept that we're all interconnected we'll stop."

This is a fine idea, but one that has a long way to go. Whilst Miller has patented his ideas for a working Celtic cross, he is yet to convince academia that ocean-going travel was commonplace from the Neolithic era.

For now, Miller's cross is largely ignored. Only time will tell if he is right.

Appendix IV

http://www.atimes.com/atimes/South_Asia/EE02Df02.html

South Asia—
India's Underwater Heritage

By Uttara Gangopadhyay

NEW DELHI—Scientists from Chennai's National Institute of Oceanography (NIO) were routinely going through some underwater sonar pictures taken while monitoring marine pollution in the Gulf of Cambay, off the coast of Gujarat, a couple of years ago. Much to their surprise, they came across the ruins of a city. Initially, the news received mixed responses. While some believed that it was the lost city of the mythical Dwarka mentioned in ancient scriptures, others dismissed it as a probable shipwreck. The scientists launched a more intensive search last year and came up with plenty of interesting finds.

The ancient city is located at a depth of 40 meters and spread over a nine-kilometer stretch with relics from a typical Indus Valley civilization—pools with sunken steps, a granary, house foundations, drainage systems, mud roads as well as broken pots, figurines, semi-precious stones, ornaments, fossilized remains of wood and human body parts. Carbon dating of wooden pieces has revealed even more interesting facts. One piece tested by the Birbal Shahni Institute of

Paleobotany in Lucknow shows it belonged to 5500 BC, while one tested by National Geophysical Research Institute, Hyderabad, belonged to 7500 BC. Although yet to be conclusively proved whether the pieces were washed to the place or belonged to the city, the findings are intriguing.

Despite its gloomy association, a shipwreck is interesting as a piece of history. It is a documentation of life on board, boat building, trade routes, cargo, etc. The wrecks turn into homes for a number of marine fauna. Divers love shipwrecks because of the challenge they offer. The luxurious ocean liner Andrea Doria that sank near Nantucket off Long Island in the Atlantic Ocean in July 1956 is now considered the "Mount Everest of shipwreck diving". Experienced divers have died in their quest to explore the ship. The UNESCO (United Nations Educational, Scientific and Cultural Organization) Convention on Underwater Cultural Heritage adopted in 2001 has now laid out a set of rules for the preservation of underwater sites and wrecks. International Heritage Day observed on April 18 had "Underwater Cultural Heritage" as its theme, aimed at raising people's awareness and to foster conservation of underwater heritage.

Throughout history, seafaring explorers have rewritten the boundaries of land many times. On the other hand, maritime trade routes have been a bone of contention between nations. The strategic location of India encouraged maritime trade and commerce as well as expeditions to foreign lands in the past. Foreigners from across the seas influenced India's history in the post-Mughal period. Hence, many people believe that the Indian seacoast can provide important shipwrecks and lost cities.

The recent findings near Mahabalipuram in Tamil Nadu seem to vindicate that belief. A joint expedition by the Scientific Exploration Society of the United Kingdom and NIO revealed an extensive series of structures at a depth of five to seven meters. The ruins, consisting of masonry walls, rock-cut structures, stone platforms with steps etc, are probably the remains of six of the seven pagodas built by the Pallava rulers. There is a popular legend among local fishermen that the beautiful city was devastated by floods unleashed by some jealous gods which caused the six pagodas to be submerged. An account by British traveler J Goldingham in 1798 referred to the place as the land of the Seven Pagodas. It was he who also recorded the myth. Some time ago, British author and television presenter Graham Hancock was inspired by the legend and it was at his initiative that the expedition took off last year.

"Despite these interesting findings, underwater exploration for archeological sites and shipwrecks is still lagging in India," feels Dr Prateep Sen of Kolkata. A certified diver, Sen often goes diving in the Southeast Asian seas. "Whether it's the flora and the fauna or heritage findings, like ancient cities and shipwrecks, the underwater world is no less interesting than the world above. The heritage findings are time capsules that lie far away from curious eyes, preserved for posterity," he says. Although the screening of the film Titanic created deeper interest in wrecks, India is yet to join the bandwagon. Mitali Kakar of Reef Watch Marine Conservation, a non-governmental organization involved in promoting diving and reef conservation, agrees, "There're several wrecks and submerged cities around the Indian subcontinent which could be landmarked as heritage sites if managed in a proper manner."

Even though underwater exploration is costly and thus difficult for individuals to finance, Sen says it is high time exploring the deep was taken seriously. "Amateur divers go down searching for hidden treasures and often come up with lovely booties." Local fishermen and boat people are well aware of such sites. Often amateur divers work on these bits of information and strike gold. "The fishermen's tales of the submerged pagodas ultimately came true in the sense that ruins were discovered here."

Sen also highlights the recent findings of a 300-year-old shipwreck now being explored by the Indian Navy off the Lakshadweep islands. "I heard about the wrecked Princess Royal lying on the seabed quite some time ago," he recalls. "It's also mentioned in the book Diving in the Indian Ocean, published in 1999 by Rizzoli of New York. According to local people, amateur divers have been down to the wreck site. The navy divers have come up with interesting findings like canons, an anchor, iron objects, porcelain as well as a bell with the ship's name inscribed on it."

Countries such as the Philippines, Indonesia and Thailand have converted shipwrecks found off their coasts into diving attractions, in the process reaping the benefits of niche tourism. The warm waters of the tropical seas are the favorite haunts of divers from all over the world and the shipwrecks have increased the attraction.

Local people reap the benefit of direct and indirect employment opportunities. According to Kakar, if the sea conditions permit visibility and people have the opportunity for scuba diving in the area, the lost city off the Gujarat coast could serve as a premier archeological site for exploration. "The income earned from this kind of eco-tourism could flow into preservation and conservation of the site and benefit the communities living along the coast."

Who would have though that the land of the famed Taj Mahal and palaces could also throw up attractions like underwater lost cities?

(Trans World Features TWF)

Appendix V

Supremely Doubtable Dogma

by James I. Nienhuis

For at least four thousand years, notions like Darwinism have swirled within the scientific and philosophic communities of the various ancient cultures of the world. An ancient Egyptian papyrus entitled *The Book of the Evolutions of Ra, and of the Overthrowing of Apepi* paints a picture of origins where all forms of life are said to have evolved from chaotic primordial waters. Similarly, the ancient Babylonian epic *Enuma Elish* describes a process by which all things evolved out of water, so obviously, these stories bear resemblance to the Darwinian theory that goo evolved into you, which is a demonstrably fallacious theory to be debunked here with a presentation of the logical alternative theory.

The Epicurean philosophers of ancient Greece were evolutionary atheists, and the Stoics of ancient Greece were evolutionary pantheists who believed that everything is God, and therefore, that everything evolves as parts of God. Aristotle believed in the spontaneous generation of non-life into life (goo to you), and he alongside Socrates and Plato believed that the universe is eternal, that it had no beginning, and thus has no Creator. Evidently, these Greek ideas were adaptations of the ancient Babylonian and Egyptian evolutionary theories which were passed-down through the writings of the eighth century B.C. Greek philosopher and historian Hesiod in his book *Theogeny.*

Plato in the fifth century B.C. proposed a structure of relative levels of life-forms through a biological categorization which is known as Plato's Chain of Being. It categorized organisms' relative levels of complexity through a prescription of simpler creatures as the lower links of the Chain of Being, with European humans at the top of the chain, just a link above non-European humans, and thusly, here is an early form of scientific racism. This framework for the categorization of life-forms became the standard by which biota were analyzed up until the time of Charles Darwin, some two-thousand two-hundred years later.

Along came Darwin with his not so original idea that the great diversities and intricacies of biological designs derived from the primordial waters through proposed causalities which cannot be observed nor falsified, Such is the plight of the Darwinists, they claim to hold unyielding truth, and yet they can demonstrate not one wit of proof for their notions, as according to Darwinism, random mutations have altered the genetic codes of creatures to such an extent that fish have morphed into lizards and lizards have morphed into birds..

Imagine if you will, a line of related lizards that supposedly suffered mutations during thousands of generations, and resultantly, embryonic wings began to develop from their front legs, so the Darwinists would have us believe that this line of lizards flopped around on the ground for thousands of generations awaiting the further mutation-driven development of their front-legs to become wings. And how did random alterations of only the germ cells (the sexually reproductive cells) by mutations cause drastic and progressive morphing of legs into more "evolutionarily advanced" appendages like wings?

Genes of sexually reproductive cells (for the next generation) are merely re-arranged or are harmed by mutations from environmental stimuli, such as radiation, chemical pollution, and perhaps magnetism, so it is unlikely that successive mutations caused a directed flow of mutation-caused morphological changes of a seemingly purposed and necessary Darwinian path for the evolution of new and higher life-forms.

Darwinian evolution is the "law of the land," and yet many hundreds of millions of people worldwide will tell you that it just doesn't pass the smell test, and Darwinists will tell you that non-Darwinian explanations of biological origins are not worthy of the light of day in academic settings. The Darwinists will say that those who are not of their ilk actually don't believe in evolution, and therefore, that those foes of Darwinism should be seen as ignorant rubes. This is a semantic fix to aid the Darwinists because creation scientists actually do believe in natural selection as evolution (that is genetic variation within animal kinds), so to say that creationists don't believe in evolution is a deliberate distortion because we do in fact believe that gene-pools have varied (naturally selected) due to the dispersion of the kinds of animals into novel ecological niches as isolated breeding groups, but we don't believe in Darwinian morphing.

The propaganda device of the semantic fixation of the generic term evolution has been used to marginalize non-Darwinian theorists, but in reality, creationists do believe in evolution per se, and not in Darwinian evolution which requires seemingly purposeful and biologically impossible maneuvers of anatomical morphing. Changes do occur in animals, for instance, there are huge varieties of dogs, from Chihuahuas to wolves, and from dingoes to French poodles, and the fact that they all are capable of interbreeding and producing offspring proves that they necessarily came from a group of common ancestors, and thusly, the so-called species that have been categorized in nature are often merely variants of an animal kind, like the various types of dogs.

Or like cats, did you know that lions and tigers can interbreed and produce offspring (ligers), or that leopards and lions can interbreed and produce offspring (leopons)? These interbreeding capabilities are indicative that they came from common ancestors, and so, observable evolution (not Darwinian evolution) is the genetic variation that occurs when the groups of the ancestor animal kinds moved off into new ecological niches in isolated breeding groups.

As a matter of fact, creatures interbreed not only at the species level on the phylogenic tree, they also can interbreed at the genus level (turtles), and even at the family level (birds), so the notion that the term species is a biologically definitive term of demarcation between types of animals is obviously ludicrous. The Darwinian evolutionary tree is based upon the idea of species, but the term species is actually meaningless because some creatures actually interbreed at the genus and family levels. The "evolution of the species" is actually and merely the genetic variations that were inevitable as ancestor animals moved off into new ecological niches in isolated breeding groups.

Mendelian characteristics flow back and forth through the gene pool of a kind of animals (e.g. cats), but they won't flow into the gene pools of different kinds (syngameons) of animals. Mendelian characteristics will not flow from cats to dogs, but they will flow quite extensively within those respective syngameons (cats and dogs). Whether Darwinian scientists like it or not, their natural selection is applicable only to genetic variation within syngameons, and not to some fanciful morphing of say lizards into birds, nor to some notion that cats and dogs came from a common distant ancestor.

Mutations do play a role in natural selection (within syngameons), they damage or merely re-arrange genetic material, but they never add genetic material for biological novelty. Mutations are notorious for their destructive effects, and their only saving grace is that they can cause a sort of shaking-up of genetic material in a creature to sometimes restore or activate some characteristics of the syngameon's gene pool, and perhaps cause something like the webbed-paws of polar bears. This effect from mutation works well for the swimming polar bears, but who would argue that the polar bear is morphing to become a fish?

The same can be said of the mutation that caused the short wings on bugs in the south Pacific, as they were then not as readily blown by the wind off the islands, so they had greater survivability, and thus, they achieved greater reproductive numbers. This is plain natural selection, it is not Darwinian natural selection where primordial goo allegedly morphed into simple one-celled organisms which then morphed into fish, and then into dinosaurs, and on into buffaloes, apes, and humans.

Darwin said that after observing the changed beak sizes of finches in the south Pacific, he was convinced that lizards evolved into birds, and that the fossil record would bear witness to his thesis that creatures have been morphing into new kinds of creatures for millions of years. Darwin admitted that the lack of evidence for Darwinian evolution in the fossil record would falsify his theory, and as it turns out, the fossil record has falsified his theory.

Fossils are entombed creatures within waterborne sedimentary layers that became petrified, and the record of the extermination of these creatures is lithified in the vast sedimentary layers of the geologic record. Because millions of fossils have been analyzed for possible missing link (transitional form) status, and because none have been determined, it is evident that Darwinian theory is on tenuous footing. In the fossil record, fish are fish, birds are birds, apes are apes, and humans are humans, and the dearth of transitional creatures in the fossil record forces Darwinian loyalists to propose rapid morphing of animals at a rate too quick to be reflected in the fossil record, this is called punctuated equilibrium, how convenient is that?

The obviously necessary punctuated equilibrium must have been in play during the Cambrian explosion, where layers usually deep in the fossil record hold fossils of simple one-cell and multi-cell marine creatures which allegedly were entombed in sediments and lithified millions of years ago when primordial goo had just begun to evolve into creatures. The obvious problem for the Darwinist here is how the inorganic material miraculously morphed into organic material, the chemistry just isn't there. But the Darwinist will snappily answer how one-celled organisms morphed into multi-celled creatures by citing punctuated equilibrium, so he would say yes, there are no fossil evidences of one-cell organisms morphing into multi-cell creatures, but you see, it happened so quickly (punctuated equilibrium) that there is no evidence that it actually ever happened.

So there you have it, magic morphing which is quicker than the eye, and many different forms of morphing like legs to wings, gills to lungs, scales to feathers, cold-blooded to warm-blooded, all having to occur with great synchronicity and seeming direction of design purpose. I go back to the supposed half-lizard/half-bird, so it flops around on the ground for thousands of generations awaiting the time when the wings (from legs) have evolved enough for the flopper to get off the ground? But wait, what about punctuated equilibrium? The Darwinist might say that there was punctuated equilibrium from legs to wings since we have no transitional fossils between lizards and birds, or he might choose to tackle the notion that the bird/lizard actually went through the flopping stage for thousands of generations. As you can see, the Darwinists have two very odd and specious response options.

The variations of the features of the members of the respective syngameons are quite extreme, for instance, the cranial capacity variation of modern humans is from seven-hundred cc to fourteen-hundred cc, so the fact that Neanderthal man and Homo erectus had cranial capacities of around fourteen-hundred cc puts them within the range of human kind, just as the thinner-headed Cro-Magnon man ranges to the lower end of the cranial-capacity spectrum of the human kind, and so, these "closer cousins" of ours were just as human as were the supposedly more primitive Neanderthal and Homo erectus humans who also lived during the Ice Age.

Relatives of the so-called woolly mammoths (which were hairy elephants) have been noted in Nepal, they have the crowned head of the woolly mammoth, and so, these are apparently the progeny of those that supposedly went extinct at the end of the Ice Age, they have survived by migrations and genetic variations within the elephant syngameon. Similarly, modern humans are the progeny of Neanderthal, Cro-Magnon, Homo erectus and Homo sapiens, as they all likely were inter-fertile, and these are merely reflections of genetic variations within the human syngameon.

The proposed missing link before Homo erectus is Australopithecus, which is actually an ape, and which could be found alive today in some remote region of the world. And the proposed missing link before Australopithecus is unknown (more punctuated equilibrium please), as the Darwinists don't want to link monkeys and humans because there are no missing links between monkeys and humans, instead, the Darwinists propose that monkeys and humans respectively morphed from a common ancestor, supposedly from some type of shrew-like creature of which there is no fossil indication, and obviously therefore, of which there are no transitional forms between the imaginary shrew-like creature and the human kind, except for the purported transitions from Australopithecus (ape), to Home erectus (human), and on to Cro-Magnon (human).

Neanderthal man doesn't even rate as a direct ancestor of modern humans because if he were properly treated as such by the Darwinists, he would correctly be seen as the tool-using, art-making, eternity-conscious human being that the evidence indicates. Neanderthal man and Homo erectus were much the same, so to try to be consistent, the Darwinists should also remove Homo erectus from the direct human family tree, which would leave only Cro-Magnon (an essentially modern human) and Australopithecus (which is an ape) as the only supposed proofs that an imaginary shrew-like creature morphed into humans over millions of generations.

And the Darwinists call that good science, and they say that if you don't believe such information then you are an unenlightened dullard who should keep his opinions to himself. Yet as the lack of transitional creatures and fossils is omnipresent, the Darwinists tenaciously hold on to their fanatic need to believe that goo morphed into you over millions of generations because of mutations (with the involvement of the ever convenient punctuated equilibrium) affecting the trial and error of life-forms in the jungle that is the survival of the fittest.

The so-called survival of the fittest is actually just a result of certain characteristics of some gene pools of creatures of a particular syngameon manifesting to allow greater survivability for those creatures in certain ecological niches. For instance, low-melanin (light-skin) people have greater survivability in the more extreme latitudes of the world, while higher-melanin (darker-skin) people have greater survivability in the middle latitudes, therefore, the so-called races of humanity are actually the manifestations of genetic variations within the human syngameon, but they are not the results of irrelevant Darwinian evolution.

It is difficult to determine the exact lines of demarcation between syngameons because variations of genetic characteristics (sometimes due to mutations) can manifest as quite profound differences in sizes, temperaments (friend or foe attitudes), and in the intra-syngameon germination capacities of the members of the different branches of the respective syngameons, and so, interbreeding between some branches of members of a syngameon (as between foxes and dogs) was practically curtailed long ago, this was after much genetic variation had already manifested in the population of the dog syngameon.

So-called speciation happened in a surprisingly few number of generations from the original ancestors of the syngameons, and such leads us to some unorthodox ideas about biological history. It seems that all of the so-called species of animals naturally selected (they did not morph) from a far fewer number of original ancestors of the respective syngameons. This is borne out from ancient history, and I will discuss such in future articles.

The original ancestors of the members of the respective syngameons were of mutt-like genetic make-ups, and thus, they carried many combinations of genes for the wide variety of characteristics which their progenies display today. It is similar that mutt-dogs will have pups of varying physical characteristics, but purebreds always breed the same kind of dog that looks virtually the same as the parents. In a manner of speaking, the varying features of the offspring of the mutts is a microcosm of that which has occurred within the syngameons through the generations since the time of their respective original ancestors.

The offspring of the mutts (and of the original syngameon members) were born with favorable characteristics and with unfavorable characteristics for survival in their environments, those with more favorable genetic features for their given environment survived to reproduce, the others did not, and as such is the process of so-called speciation within the syngameons, and that is genetic variation and natural selection within the respective syngameons, it is not Darwinian evolution.

Yet scientists and educators of Darwinism get away with saying that creationists don't believe in evolution, when in fact, as stated before, creationists do believe in evolution as natural selection within the syngameons. We do not believe in Darwinian evolution which says that mutations caused creatures to morph into new kinds of creatures, so obviously, it is Darwinian evolution that is at issue here, and not at issue is whether or not creationists believe in evolution, as we do see validity in natural selection and genetic variation within the respective syngameons, but not across syngameons, so let's call it evolution, but let's not call it Darwinian evolution.

The semantic fixation by the scientific establishment that creationists don't believe in evolution has been a powerful tool to prevent the presentation of alternatives to Darwinian evolution in the schools. If proponents of alternative theories to Darwinian evolution want to be taken seriously, we must let people know that we do believe in evolution per se, but we don't believe in Darwinian evolution which preaches that impossible biochemical changes have caused inorganic material to morph into organisms, and that have caused insects to morph into fish, and lizards into birds, and imaginary shrew-like creatures into humans, and it makes you want to scream.

The Georgia school system recently discussed whether or not a proviso should be added to the teaching of evolution that it is just a theory and not a fact, and that it has major weaknesses of which the students should be made aware. That's all well and good, except that the material under discussion should rightly be called Darwinian evolution, it should not be generically labeled evolution because almost everyone agrees that evolution (natural selection within syngameons) is a fact of biology, but by using the generic term evolution (instead of Darwinian evolution) in the debate, the Darwinists are able to demonize the opposition by saying that the proponents of the alternative models of biological origins don't even believe in evolution, and therefore, that because evolution is all that is legitimate regarding biological origins, you should not mess with the only real theory that can rationalize biological origins, so forget about the alternative theories.

Do you see the semantic fix which is in play? Opponents of the exclusive teaching of Darwinian theory as fact to our children should realize that this is a semantic game. We need to define the terms, as evolution per se is much different from pie-in-the-sky Darwinian evolution, and the distinction between the two must be noted and properly labeled in order to effectively debate the merits of Darwinian evolution vis-à-vis generic evolution (which is natural selection within the syngameons). The generic term evolution should rightly be seen as not synonymous with the term Darwinian evolution, if this proper distinction is not acknowledged by all, then the Darwinian monolith will continue to dominate our education systems.

Darwinists often argue that an allowance of the teaching of alternative theories regarding biological origins in the classrooms would cause some kind of dumbing-down of the students' powers of logic and rationality, when in reality, the presentation of such as that which I have here in part presented would cause the students to think and properly consider the vast linkages of animals within the respective syngameons, and they would thus be more aware of the hybridization potentials between so-called species. And the presentation of this model would cause the students to desire to investigate the limits of the respective syngameons, and therefore, such investigations would be the practice of good science by and for our students.

I spent about a year on the New York Times message board under the category Human Origins discussing anthropology, geology, Darwinian evolution (and how creationists do in fact believe in evolution per se), and discussing the origins of the human kind with my not so kindly foes who were almost all Darwinian liberals. They consistently maintained that an allowance of the presentation of alternative (not Darwinian) theories in the schools would cause the students to lose their appreciation for the scientific method, and would cause them to not think logically thereafter, and thus, our future leaders would not produce any new ideas for scientific progress which my foes say derive from Darwinian theory, as if productive studies in chemistry, geology, astronomy, engineering, and medicine are somehow predicated upon a mysterious Darwinian matrix.

I asked my intellectual foes what scientific breakthroughs could be cited that reveal the supposed Darwinian underpinnings of all good science? After much prodding, they finally came up with two incredibly impotent examples to support their position, traffic-flow solutions and improved airplane wing designs. So there you have it, the best examples of the alleged Darwinian matrix which should rightly underpin all quests for scientific innovation. As you can see, Darwinian theory has essentially no bearing on the trains of thought which are inherent in scientists' quests for innovations, and so, the notion that the presentation of non-Darwinian theories about biological origins in the classroom would somehow destroy our potential for future innovations is patently absurd.

And the supposed Darwinian evolution of an imaginary shrew-like creature to become (not through monkeys) the members of the human syngameon is be accepted without question, and without question because the Darwinian monolith says that it is so, and because creationists allegedly don't believe in evolution, and therefore, should have no say in these matters. But the prime supposed evidences for the morphing of humankind from an imaginary shrew-like creature fall into one of three categories, fully human, fully ape, or fully and demonstrably fraudulent.

For instance, one of the classic supposed examples of the Darwinian evolution of the human kind is Piltdown man, however, this alleged creature which has been championed as a prime example of proof for the Darwinian evolution of humans was actually a combination of a human skull and an ape jaw, of which plaster casts where made, and the casts were mailed off to and accepted by the great centers of learning of the world. Another alleged missing link known as Nebraska man was later determined to have been a creative rendering based upon what turned out to be only a pig's tooth, that's right folks, a misidentified pig's tooth gave the Darwinists reason to think that they had found another supposed missing link, such are the depths to which Darwinists will sink to vainly uphold their dogma.

The infamous supposed missing link named Lucy which was discovered by Louis Leakey is actually just an ape (or a chimp), and the other imagined missing links that have also been cited in the literature are also purely ape, or purely human, or purely fraudulent, and please know that humans and apes are not of the same syngameon, so there obviously will continue to be no evidence of a genetic connection between the two in the fossil record.

It seems that the genetic variations within the human syngameon have been ongoing for a surprisingly short period of time. Studies of Y chromosome variations within the male human population show that the earliest male ancestor of today's men lived only thousands of years ago. The rate of Y chromosome variations among males through history may have been more rapid than first calculated, so the earliest male ancestor of ours could have lived only a few thousand years ago. And the variation of mitochondrial DNA in women has been measured, the results suggest that the measured variation occurred within one to ten thousand generations, however, the confidence level for that probability-spread is ninety-five percent, so straying into the remaining five percent, the earliest female ancestor of the human syngameon may also have lived only a few thousand years ago.

Noteworthy is the fact that within the fossil record, humans are humans, apes are apes, shrews are shrews, but allegedly, hundreds of millions of years before the supposed morphing of the shrew, Darwinian dogmatists describe imaginary water creatures which supposedly morphed to become frogs, snails, snakes, lizards, turtles, and other swamp denizens, as biological life was allegedly evolving out from the water. However, fossils which according to mainstream scientists were formed hundreds of millions of years ago do not include possible ancestors of the frogs, snails, snakes, and turtles which in the fossil record look little different than today's versions of those creatures.

Why did they stay the same through the imagined hundreds of millions of years of so-proposed natural morphing, and why is there no evidence of any evolutionary ancestors of the frogs, snails, snakes, turtles, and of all the other animals in the fossil record? It is because they are members of respective syngameons which have genetic capacity limitations, such as horses will not breed cows. The genetic limits of the respective syngameons merits further investigation, but it is obvious that vast numbers of so-called species are actually inter-fertile and thus are members of larger syngameons (like llamas, camels, and alpacas are of one syngameon). In the fossil record, fish are fish, birds are birds, clams are clams, and reptiles are reptiles, so the drumbeat of all that morphing is definitely a ruse.

It is time that we articulate the nuance that creationists do in fact believe in evolution (per se), but we don't believe in Darwinian evolution. Natural selection is merely a term for the genetic variation that has occurred within the respective syngameons because groups of ancestor animals of each syngameon moved off into disparate ecological niches as isolated breeding groups, therefore, evolution is not a term to be claimed exclusively for Darwinian theorists.

Actually, Darwinian morphing has nothing to do with the observable "speciation" within syngameons, but it has everything to do with magical morphing and punctuated equilibrium (abracadabra). So since natural selection is a term for genetic variation which can be demonstrated to have occurred within syngameons, and since Darwinism with its punctuated equilibrium is merely fancy and of no practical use, perhaps the utilization of the term natural selection should be reserved for only creationists. We do believe in evolution per se, and science bears out natural selection within the respective syngameons, but creationists don't believe in Darwinian evolution which goes way beyond natural selection into the realms of punctuated equilibrium, magical morphing, and no evidence whatsoever that those ever happened.

Humankind is not presently morphing into new syngameons of creatures (look out for magical punctuated equilibrium), but we are breeding freely amongst the advertised races of humanity, so new combinations of human syngameon genes are predictably evident in the human population, and new genetic links between "species" (hybrids) are discovered consistently, such is the evidence for natural (or induced) selection within the syngameons, and such are the reasons why alternative theoretical models for biological evolution should be presented to our students.

For the sake of intellectual honesty, and for the sake of good science, viable alternatives to Darwinian theory should be presented to the public at large and to the students in general because the Darwinian model is scientifically laughable, and because an alternative theory such as that summarized herewith has much explanatory power, whereas, overly-hyped Darwinian dogma explains nothing, and that is why Darwinian theory has been dubbed the Supremely Doubtable Dogma.

James I. Nienhuis is an author and lecturer,
his website is http://www.GenesisVeracity.com.

End Notes

Chapter 1

1. Graham Hancock, *Underworld* (New York, New York, Crown Publishing, 2002), p. 675. http://www.hindunet.org/saraswati/khambat/khambat01.htm.
2. *Underworld,* op. cit.
3. Ibid, 214.
4. Dr M. Sundaram, Head of the Department of Tamil studies, Presidency College, Madras, "The Cultural Heritage of the Ancient Tamils," research paper.
5. C. Ramachandran Dikshitar, Studies in Tamil Literature and History, chapter 1, (Madras, The South India Sauiva Siddhanta Works Publishing Society, 1983).
6. Hancock, op. cit. 252.
7. Ibid, 152.
8. Ibid, 688.
9. http://www.GrahamHancock.com.
10. Information from Professor Massaaki Kimura, marine geologist at the University of Ryuku: http://www.lauralee.com/japan.htm.
11. http://www.s8int.com/water6.html. (great pictures at this site of various submerged megaliths, you can search engine it under Ooparts & Ancient High Technology)
12. Hancock, op. cit., 17.
13. Ibid, 18.
14. http://hometown.aol.com/ibss1/page2/.
15. Hancock, op. cit., 19.

Chapter 2

None.

Chapter 3

1. Charles H. Hapgood, *Maps of the Ancient Sea Kings* (Kempton, Illinois, Adventures Unlimited Press, 1996 ed.), p. 82.
2. Graham Hancock, Underworld (New York, New York, Crown Publishing, 2002), p. 477.
3. Hapgood, op. cit., p. 20.
4. Ibid, p. 171.
5. Ibid, p. 69.
6. Hancock, op. cit., p. 663.

Chapter 4

1. Graham Hancock, *Fingerprints of the Gods* (New York, New York, Three Rivers Press, 1995), p. 247.
2. *Feats and Wisdom of the Ancients* (Time Life Books, 1990), p. 65.
3. *Egyptian Book of the Dead* (trans. E. A. Wallis Budge), British Museum, 1895; (London and New York, Arkana, 1986), Introduction, p. L.
4. http://www.livius.org/a/iran/persepolis/apadana/apadana.html.
5. Hancock, op. cit., p. 261.
6. http://www.indhistory.com/hindu-temple/hindu-temple-dwarka-temple.html.
   http://www.indiansaga.info/temples/dwarka_temple.html.
7. Gustav Schlegel, *The Hung League* (Scotland, Tynron Press, 1990), Introduction, XXXVII.
8. Hancock, op. cit., 260.

Chapter 5

1. Rosalie David, *Religions and Magic in Ancient Egypt* (New York, New York, Penguin Books, 2002), p. 75.
2. R. O. Faulkner (translator), *The Ancient Egyptian Pyramid Texts*, (Oxford University Press, 1969), numerous utterances such as 248, 268, and 570 where the king says "I am a star which illumines the sky."
   Rosalie David, *Religion and Magic in Ancient Egypt* (London, England, Penguin Books, 2001), p. 90.

3. http://zebu.uoregon.edu/~imamura/121/lecture-2/nabta.html.
4. http://southport.jpl.nasa.gov/reports/finrpt/McCauley/mccauley.htm.
5. David Hatcher Childress, *Lost Cities of Africa and Asia* (Kempton, Illinois, Adventures Unlimited Press, 1991), check index or Sahara portion of book.
6. http://zebu.uoregon.edu/~imamura/121/lecture-2/nabta.html

7. Woolley 1929: "*The Sumerians*," by Charles Leonard Woolley (New York, New York, W. W. Norton, 1929, 1965 reprint; Barnes and Noble 1995 reprint) http://www.iranian.com/History/2005/March/Gutians/.
8. http://www.newindpress.com/sunday/colItems.asp?ID=SEC20020817100019 http://www.hindunet.org/saraswati/khambat/khambat01.htm
9. Graham Hancock, *Underworld* (New York, New York, Crown Publishers, 1995), p. 123.
10. Ralph T. Griffith (translator), *Hymns of the Rig Veda*, volume 1 (Delhi, India,Munisharam Manoharlal Publishers, 1987), footnote 99.
11. Ibid, vol. 2, 44, 6.
12. Graham Hancock, *Fingerprints of the Gods* (New York, New York, Three Rivers Press, 1995), 422-423.
13. Ibid, p. 346.
14. Ibid, p. 422.

Chapter 6

1. Giorgio de Santillana and Hertha de von Dechend, *Hamlet's Mill* (Boston, David R. Godine, 1992). http://phoenixandturtle.net/excerptmill/santillana.htm
2. Ralph T. Griffin (transl.), *Hymns of the Rgveda*, vol I, 318 and 319, Munisharam Manoharlal Publishers, Delhi, 1987 (first published in 1889).
3. Ibid, hymn 104.
4. http://www.arcane-archive.org/interdisciplinary/numbers/sl-108-1.php

Chapter 7

1. Peter Tompkins, *Mysteries of the Mexican Pyramids* (London, Thames & Hudson, 1987), p. 347.
2. *Popol Vuh: The Sacred Book of the Ancient Quiche Maya,* English version by Delia Goetz and S.G. Morley from the translation by Adrian Recinos, (University of Oklahoma Press, 1991), p. 178.
3. Ibid, p. 168-169.
4. Graham Hancock, *Fingerprints of the Gods* (New York, New York, Three Rivers Press, 1995), p. 260.
5. http://www.orion.it.luc.edu/~cwinter/priest2.htm
6. http://www.waiscores.dri.edu/individual.html
7. http://www.waiscores.dri.edu/individual.html
8. http://www.delange.org/LaVenta5/LaVenta5.htm
9. http://www.raceandhistory.com/historicalviews/ancientamerica.htm

10. *Venidad*, Fargard I, cited in Lokamanya Bal Gangadhar Tilak, *The Arctic Home in the Vedas* (Poona, India, Tilak Publishers, 1956), pp. 340-341.
11. Cited from *The Mythology of South America in* Graham Hancock, *Fingerprints of the Gods* (New York, New York, Three Rivers Press, 1995), p. 202.
12. Ibid., p. 65.
13. Graham Hancock, *Underworld* (New York, New York, Crown Publishing, 2002), p. 178.
14. Michael J. Oard, *An Ice Age Caused by the Genesis Flood* (El Cajon, California, Institute for Creation Research, 1990), p. 63.
15. http://cc.msnscache.com/cache.aspx?q=1733854301378&lang=en-US&FORM=CVRE2
16. Hancock, op. cit., p. 126.
17. http://kuyper.calvin.edu/s/scaff/encyc/encyc01/htm/iii.ix.ii.htm

Chapter 8

1. http://kuyper.calvin.edu/s/schaff/encyc/encyc01/htm/iii.ix.ii.htm
2. http://www.awarenessquest.com/osborn.htm
   http://wwwksonline.com/pob/pob_ch17.html
3. Ibid.
4. *Feats and Wisdom of the Ancients* (Time-Life Books, 1990), p.65.
5. http://www.stonepages.com/news/archives/000166.html
6. Graham Hancock, *The Message of the Sphinx* (New York, New York,Three Rivers Press, 1996), p. 64.
7. Egyptian Book of the Dead (trans. E. A. Wallis Budge), British Museum, 1895, (London and New York, Arkana, 1986), Introduction, p l through liv.
8. http://kuyper.calvin.edu/s/schaff/encyc/encyc01/htm/iii.ix.ii.htm
9. http://orion.it.luc.edu/~cwinter/priest2.htm
10. http://www.sogol.com?WHP/IINFO/Ready%20%20INT/SUSA/Susa%20web.htm
11. http://www.livius.org/a/iran/persepolis/apadana/apadana.html
12. The Kaldis were noted “magicians,” the followers of Kaldi, son of Arphaxad.
13. http://www.crystalinks.com/amphibiousgods.html
14. http://www.xleb.com/heritage/skanda/dionysus.htm
15. Ibid.
16. Edmund Sollberger, *The Babylonian Legend of the Flood* (London, British Museum Publications, 1984), p. 26.
17. Hancock, op. cit, p. 41.
18. Graham Hancock, *Underworld* (New York, New York, Crown Publishers, 2002), p. 556.
19. Ibid, p. 553-560.

20. Ibid, p. 553-560.
21. Post Wheeler, *The Sacred Scriptures of the Japanese* (Henry Schuman Inc., 1952), p. 93.
22. Hancock, op. cit., p. 564.
23. http://www.yomirui.co.jp/newse/20041207wp61/htm
24. Ibid.

Chapter 9

1. http://lauralee.com/japan.htm
2. Charles Hapgood, *Maps of the Ancient Sea Kings* (Kempton, Illinois, Adventures Unlimited Press, 1996), p. 184.
3. Graham Hancock, *Underworld* (New York, New York, Crown Publishers, 2002), p. 461.
4. Ibid, p. 498.
5. http://www.kitombo.com/e/gimon/0204.html
6. W. J. Perry, *The Children of the Sun* (Kempton, Illinois, Adventures Unlimited Press, 1923), pp. 23-30.
7. Hancock, op. cit., p. 573
8. http://www.chilit.org/MUMFORD4.HTM
9. http://www.affs.org/html/ryukyuan_landforms.html
10. Ibid.
11. Graham Hancock, *Fingerprints of the Gods* (New York, New York, Three Rivers Press, 1995), p. 219.
12. Hancock, op. cit., p. 445.
13. Ibid, p. 50-80.
14. Ibid, p. 79.
15. Perry, op. cit., much of the book.
16. Ibid.
17. Posnanasky, Arthur, *Tiahuanacu: The Cradle of American Man, vol. III* (New York, New York, J. J. Augustin, 1945), pp. 142-143.
18. Quaternary Extinction: A Prehistoric Revolution, Paul S. Martin, Richard G. Klein, eds., The University of Arizona Press, 1984, p. 85.
19. Perry, op. cit.
20. Ibid, p. 23.
21. Ibid, p. 24.

Chapter 10

1. http://www.awarenessquest.com/osborn.htm
2. http://www.jrbooksonline.com/pob/pob_ch17.html
3. Ibid.

4. Ralph Ellis, *Thoth, Architect of the Universe* (Dorset, England, Edfu Books, 1998), p. 13.
5. Charles Leonard Woolley, *Woolley 1929: "The Sumerians"* (New York, New York, W. W. Norton, 1929, 1965 reprint; reprint Barnes and Noble, 1995). http://www.iranian.com/History/2005/March/Gutians/.
6. Mageoghagan, C. 1627. The Annals of Clonmacnoise. Printed in Dublin at University Press. 1896. (Murphy ed.), p. 13.
7. Bill Cooper, *After the Flood* (West Sussex, England, New Wine Press, 1995), p. 252.

Chapter 11

1. http://www.chn.ir/english/eshownews.asp?no=4740
2. http://studentweb.tulane.edu/~plal/mohenjo-daro.html

Chapter 12

1. Graham Hancock, *Fingerprints of the Gods* (New York, New York, Three Rivers Press, 1995), pp. 187-198.
   Sir J. G. Frazer, *Folklore in the Old Testament: Studies in Comparative Religion, Legend and Law* (abridged edition, London, Macmillan, 1923).
2. Hancock, op. cit., p. 188-189.
3. http://www.custance.org/Library/Volume9/Part_II/chapter2.html
4. http://www.xuquang.com/english/hoiane1.htm
5. http://custance.org/old/seed/appebd.html
6. Hancock, op. cit., p. 81 (from Fragments of Berosus, from Alexander Polyhistor).
7. http://web.austin.utexas.edu/edcannon/astro-climate.htm
8. Michael J. Oard, *An Ice Age Caused by the Genesis Flood* (San Diego, Calif. Institute for Creation Research, 1990).
9. Hancock, op. cit., p. 197 (cited from Egyptian Book of the Dead)
10. E. A. Wallis Budge (transl.), *The Egyptian Book of the Dead* (Mineola, New York, Dover Publications, 1967), Introduction, p. xciv.
11. Ibid, xcix.
12. E. A. E. Reymond, *The Mythical Origin of the Egyptian Temple* (New York, New York, Manchester University Press, Barnes and Noble Press Inc., 1969).
13. Budge, op. cit., Introduction cxxxv.
14. Ibid. p. 256.
15. http://www.themystica.org/mythical-folk/articles/Baal.htm
16. Graham Hancock, *Underworld* (New York, New York, Crown Publishers, 1995), p. 27.

17. Graham Hancock, *The Message of the Sphinx* (New York, New York, Three Rivers Press, 1996), p. 350.
18. Hancock, *Fingerprints of the Gods*, op. cit., p. 190.
19. Michael J. Oard, *An Ice Age Caused by the Genesis Flood* (El Cajon, Calif., Institute for Creation Research).

Chapter 13

1. Jack Cuozzo, *Buried Alive* (Green Forest, Arkansas, Master Books, 1998).
2. Marvin L. Lubenow, *Bones of Contention* (Grand Rapids, Michigan, Baker Books, 1992).
3. http://www.us-israel.org/jsource/Archaeology/carmel.html
4. Graham Hancock, *Underworld* (New York, New York, Crown Publishers, 2002), p. 178.
5. Larry Pierce, "In the Days of Peleg," Creation Ex Nihilo, vol. 22, no. 1 (2000), p. 46.
6. Lubenow, op. cit., p. 143.
7. Ibid.
8. Ibid., p. 149.
9. Ibid.
10. http://www.sogaer.ex.ac.uk/archaeology/research/doggerland.shtml
11. http://www.chilit.org/MUMFORD4.HTM
12. W. J. Perry, *The Children of the Sun* (Kempton, Illinois, Adventures Unlimited Press, 2004 edition of 1923 original), pp. 141-145.
13. Graham Hancock, *Fingerprints of the Gods* (New York, New York, Three Rivers Press, 1995), pp. 171-173.
    http://www.world-mysteries.com/mpl_7.htm
14. Ibid.
15. http://www.rocklakeresearch.com/history.htm
16. http://www.orion.it.luc.edu/~cwinter/priest2.htm
    http://www.orion.it.luc.edu/~cwinter/art1.html
17. http://www.msnbc.com/news/967545.asp

Chapter 14

1. E. A. Wallis Budge (transl.), *The Egyptian Book of the Dead* (Mineola, New York, Dover Publications, 1967), p. 187.
2. E. A. E. Reymond, *The Mythical Origin of the Egyptian Temple* (Manchester, England, Manchester University Press, Barnes and Noble Inc., New York, New York, 1969), p. 59.
3. R. T. Rundle Clark, *Myth and Symbol in Ancient Egypt* (London, England, Thames and Hudson, 1991), p. 246.

4. http://pubs.usgs.gov/publications/text/developing.html
5. Reymond, op. cit., p. 59.
6. Budge, op. cit., p. 123.
7. Ibid., p. 256.
8. Larry Pierce, "In the Days of Peleg," Creation Ex Nihilo, vol. 22, no. 1 (2000), p. 46.
9. Fragments of Berossus, from Alexander Polyhistor in: Graham Hancock, *Fingerprints of the Gods* (New York, New York, Three Rivers Press, 1995), p. 81.
10. W. J. Perry, *The Children of the Sun* (Kempton, Illinois, Adventures Unlimited Press, 1923), p. 146.
11. Ibid., p. 133.
12. Ibid., p. 258.
13. Ibid., p. 159
14. Ibid., p. 175.
15. Ibid., pp. 205-210.
16. Zahi Hawass and Mark Lehner, "The Sphinx: Who Built It and Why?" in *Archaeology*, Sept-Oct. 1994, p. 34.
17. Larry Pierce, op. cit.
18. Graham Hancock, *Fingerprints of the Gods* (New York, New York, Three Rivers Press, 1995), p. 438.

Chapter 15

1. W.J. Perry, *Children of the Sun* (Kempton, Illinois, Adventures Unlimited Press, 2004), pp. 205-210.
2. R. T. Rundle Clark, *Myth and Symbol in Ancient Egypt* (London, England, Thames and Hudson, 1991), p. 108.
3. Graham Hancock and Robert Bauval, The Message of the Sphinx (New York, New York, Three Rivers Press, 1996, from Pyramid Texts), p. 164.
4. Hancock, Bauval, op. cit., p. 172.
5. Ibid, (from Pyramid Texts), p. 156.
6. Ibid., p. 163.
7. Rosalie David, *Religion and Magic in Ancient Egypt* (London, England, Penguin Books), p. 319.
8. R. T. Rundle Clark, op. cit., p. 109.